The Gift of Adult ADD

How to Transform your Challenges & Build on your Strengths

By
Lara Honos-Webb, Ph.D.

16
EasyRead Large

RHYW

Copyright Page from the Original Book

Publisher's Note

This publication is designed to provide accurate and authoritative information in regard to the subject matter covered. It is sold with the understanding that the publisher is not engaged in rendering psychological, financial, legal, or other professional services. If expert assistance or counseling is needed, the services of a competent professional should be sought.

Distributed in Canada by Raincoast Books

New Harbinger Publications, Inc.
5674 Shattuck Avenue
Oakland, CA 94609
www.newharbinger.com

Printed in the United States of America

Acquired by Tesilya Hanauer; Cover design by Amy Shoup;
Edited by Amy Johnson; Text design by Tracy Carlson

Library of Congress Cataloging-in-Publication Data

Honos-Webb, Lara.
The gift of adult ADD : how to transform your challenges and build on your strengths / Lara Honos Webb.
p. cm.
Includes bibliographical references.
ISBN-13: 978-1-57224-565-5 (pbk. : alk. paper)
ISBN-10: 1-57224-565-4 (pbk. : alk. paper) 1. Attention-deficit disorder in adults--Popular works. I. Title.
RC394.A85H66 2008
616.85'89--dc22

2008029811

10 09 08

10 9 8 7 6 5 4 3 2 1

First printing

Set in 16 pt. Verdana

TABLE OF CONTENTS

"Lara Honos-Webb shows us how the demands of a global and digital culture may make the signature traits of ADD—inventiveness, need for stimulation, and interpersonal intuition—in high demand."

—Daniel H. Pink, author of *A Whole New Mind*

"If you have ADD and have been looking for the meaning of your struggles, this book will change your life. You will see, beyond doubt, that it's time to stop patching up your weaknesses and start learning about your many gifts."

—Carol Adrienne, Ph.D., author of *The Purpose of Your Life*

"Honos-Webb's book is a wonderful guidebook for optimistic living. What one chooses to focus on grows, and Honos-Webb has provided the framework for others to learn this important philosophy. It is especially important for those with ADHD to embrace the positive side of their personalities."

—Stephanie Moulton Sarkis, Ph.D., author of *Making the Grade with ADD* and 10 *Simple Solutions to Adult ADD*

"In her newest book, Honos-Webb builds on the core principles of her previous work to show how adults with ADD can find fulfilling and rewarding lives by *being who they are.* 'Find what you love and are good at, and let that guide you,' she advises, offering real-life stories of people who have done just that. In this inspiring book, Honos-Webb provides a host of specific activities to help adults with ADD use self-reflection, insight, and creativity to address weaknesses without letting those weaknesses overshadow their strengths and talents. *The Gift of Adult ADD* is a welcome addition to the growing body of literature that shows how to go beyond limiting—and misleading—diagnostic labels."

—Barbara Probst, MSW, LCSW, author of *When the Labels Don't Fit*

"A revolutionary, paradigm-shifting book that will undoubtedly change the way we think about ADD. Honos-Webb's contribution is a gift, providing no-nonsense strategies and inspiring examples of how to transform apparent deficits into strengths and assets."

—Kelly Howell, president, Brain Sync

"Talk about a gift! This book will be a true gift for anyone with ADD. While it can be discouraging to live with ADD, Honos-Webb's wise and helpful book will show readers how to use their ADD to *improve* their relationships and work lives. She then goes on to identify and explain the five specific gifts that adult ADD brings. This wonderful book has the power to transform the life and consciousness of anyone dealing with ADD."

—Mira Kirshenbaum, author of *When Good People Have Affairs, Too Good to Leave, Too Bad to Stay,* and *Everything Happens for a Reason*

"Are you ready to let this precious volume transform you, your world, and your 'adult attention deficit disorder'? Here is a gift that can be magical and life changing, both for you and your 'adult attention deficit disorder.'"

—Alvin R. Mahrer, Ph.D., professor emeritus at the University of Ottawa, author of *The Manual of Optimal Behaviors*

This book is dedicated to Ken, Kenny, and Audrey Webb for giving me the gift of waking up happy every day.

Acknowledgments

I can't find the words to express the love and gratitude deep in my heart for Karen, John, Ed, Chrissty, Grace, and Catherine Honos for their love and support. Thanks to Carole and Bill Webb, and Anna, Rosanna, and Dale Chalfant for their constant encouragement and occasional babysitting.

This book owes everything to those who shared their stories. I feel like all of you are lifetime friends. Thanks to Kimberly McCoy for being a sister soul and leadership coach for me. I hate to think what this book would be without the steady inspiration from Steve Prevett; thanks to him for opening his story and letting his family be included in this book—and for the Monty Python consultation. Captain Scott Ohlrich's brilliant mind contributed enormously to my understanding of creativity and also gave me my favorite visual image of a person with ADD: "Who else could stand on the roof of a burning house in an icy rainstorm and laugh at how they have 'the greatest job in the world'?" I am eternally grateful to Paul Orfalea for his courage in sharing his story, and to his staff and students for a fascinating collection of stories about this remarkable man. Brian Rocha's sweet generosity, wise consultation, engaging dinner conversation, free meal with all calories accounted for, and invitation to Rochapalooza were some of my favorite gifts received in writing this book. Damon

Harper's steady influx of warmth and encouragement and upbeat sharing has been a bright light for me throughout this process. I can't think of Hagen without adding in my own mind, "Hagen the hilarious"; thanks for being so memorable and sharing so much for this book. You've become a top-shelf friend and incredible collaborator on education before medication. It was with great delight that I was joined by Dr. Stephanie Moulton Sarkis. I thank her for her expert and personal contribution to this book; it was a joy to travel with a fellow writer. And finally, I am awed by Bill Jacobs Jr.'s dedication to the families who struggle with ADD and his own profound contribution to the field. I will also always remember the illuminating conversation with Marc Allen and his wonderful example of breaking down limiting beliefs. Thanks also to Steve Brown, both for his story and for giving me the idea of presenting a series of profiles.

Last, but certainly not least, I am grateful to my former student "Mike"; I can never express the depth of my debt to him for kick-starting the gift of ADD revolution in my mind. How far our ideas have come is a testament to his own great gifts. And thanks, too, to "Vishnu," for his generous and brilliant contribution, for traveling on the same wavelength, thinking and talking at the speed of light, and for playing the quantum field to such never-before-seen effect.

I'd like to thank all the same folks and mentors I acknowledged in my first book with New Harbinger, *The Gift of ADHD,* especially Tesilya Hanauer, Melissa Kirk, Heather Mitchener, Lorna Garano, Troy DuFrene, and Earlita Chenault, who I appreciate more and more with each book. Amy Johnson's spectacular editing saved the day once again.

Thanks to my mom-buddies and their husbands and children for nourishing my family and soul.

Thanks to Marc and Janet Celentana, Cy Estonactac, and Jenny Yeaggy for fond memories of must-see TV and other adventures.

I will be eternally grateful to Dick and Alison Jones and their family for their remarkable generosity of spirit. Without the lifelong support of John Thomas I could never have made so many of my dreams come true.

I'd like to thank Kelly Howell for her friendship, support, and breakthrough healing technologies. I'm forever grateful to Carol Adrienne for her coaching and continued support. Thanks to Dr. Al Mahrer for being an inspiration and exactly the revolutionary the world needs now. Thanks to Deborah Harper for inviting me into the world of podcasting. I'm grateful to the inspired book coaching of Bruce Gelfand.

Thanks to all of my clients for sharing their mysteries with me. You are my primary inspiration.

And finally, thanks to the most important people in the world—nannies and teachers: To Molly McCann and Toni and Christina Douglass, for their loving care of Kenny and Audrey. To Miss Sapna, Miss Asya, Miss Ann, and Miss Sheila for being bright lights in the lives of my kids.

Introduction

A radio show host once described my first book, *The Gift of ADHD* (2005), as applying the principles of the runaway best seller *The Secret* (Byrne 2006). While I am a fan of the basic ideas in *The Secret,* I felt defensive enough to explain that my book was published before *The Secret.* As a well-trained psychologist, I was afraid that my approach—applying clinical observation, sound theory, and established research on the power of self-fulfilling prophesies and optimism to understanding ADHD and ADD—would be trivialized as a spin-off of a popular fad.

But I am struck by one important lesson that can be derived from *The Secret's* law of attraction. According to the law of attraction, what you see in the present is created by the past. If you define reality by what you see in the present, you create a future that will be no different. If you want a different future, you have to change your perception of what you actually see now.

This simple idea addresses one of the biggest challenges of applying the ideas detailed in *The Gift of ADHD* and *The Gift of Adult ADD.* Sometimes people with ADHD or ADD have such out-of-control symptoms that they don't believe any gifts are present. To recognize and understand these gifts, you must first suspend your disbelief. You may look around you and see relationships difficulties, professional failures, and a trail of catastrophic mistakes caused by sloppiness.

It is here that you must embrace the idea that what you're presently seeing is created in part by *not* seeing the gifts. Finding and focusing on the gifts will create a different future for you. So, if you're tempted to doubt, remember: Changing the way you see yourself will change you and your life. Don't allow yourself to be distracted or derailed by what you see around you now.

ADD AND ADHD

You may be wondering what ADD is and how it differs from ADHD. ADD stands for attention deficit disorder, ADHD for attention-deficit/hyperactivity disorder. In my previous books, I used ADHD because that is the precise diagnostic term presently used in the bible of the field, *The Diagnostic and Statistical Manual of Mental Disorders* (American Psychiatric Association [APA] 2000). Not only is ADD not, as of 2007, listed in this manual, the current system defines ADHD as a *developmental* disorder and does not presently include criteria for diagnosing adults. (The most authoritative method for diagnosing adult ADD is covered in chapter 1.)

In this book, I've chosen to use ADD rather than ADHD because the hyperactivity component tends to be less troublesome for adults than it is for kids. Also, the term ADD is more widely used in the lay world, and thus more recognizable. It's also less of a mouthful to say and read.

FLEXIBLE THINKING

As you read this book, I challenge you to practice flexible thinking. If an idea presented contradicts something you've heard elsewhere, rather than rigidly arguing about which viewpoint must be the correct one, ask yourself, "Is there a way both of these could be true?" For example, this book invites you to think optimistically about who you are and what you are capable of. You may at times resist this invitation, worrying that if you think only of the positive you won't take responsibility for impulsive behaviors. Ask yourself, "Is there a way I can reframe my impulsiveness and still take responsibility for my behavior?" Push yourself to find ways to think in terms of "both-and" rather than "either-or."

Similarly, when you hear that you need to find a career that honors your ADD style, you may think, "Are you telling me I need to lower my standards?" No. Again, push yourself to find ways that you can both honor your ADD *and* raise your standards. There is no reason you can't do both. In practice, as you stop trying to cram yourself into a mold that doesn't work for you, you'll move from simply fulfilling performance demands toward becoming a genius in your arena of interest.

HOW TO USE THIS BOOK

Each chapter of this book contains one or more activities to help you learn more about yourself and apply the book's ideas to your life. Since you have ADD, you will be tempted to skip over these. That's fine, but if you want to make actual changes in your life, know that these activities will pay off. Consider buying yourself a special journal to use as you go through the book, both to work through these activities and to write your thoughts and ideas in.

Each chapter also includes an inspirational story of someone who has achieved success not just in spite of but because of having ADD. Individuals profiled include Kimberly McCoy, a psychotherapist; Steve Prevett, a successful businessman; Scott Ohlrich, a fire captain; Paul Orfalea, the founder of Kinko's; Bill Jacobs Jr., a successful business owner; Damon Harper, a physical trainer and coach; Hagen, another successful entrepreneur; and Stephanie Moulton Sarkis, a writer and psychologist. I've also included the stories of "Mike," a student of mine, and "Vishnu," a client.

I didn't record these interviews but have included some re-creations of our conversations to give you a flavor of the live-action ADD style—often wildly tangential and impulse driven. If you ever need a boost, revisit the profiles of these amazing real people.

HOW THIS BOOK IS LAID OUT

In chapter 1 we will review the specific symptoms of adult ADD. You will learn that while you may have ADD, you are much more than your ADD. While acknowledging the dark side of an ADD diagnosis, this chapter will begin to paint a picture for you of the bright side of ADD.

Chapter 2 will help you recognize that the most important thing you can do to cope with your ADD is to find the right environment—one that matches your profile of gifts and weaknesses. You will also learn that you don't have to do everything well. Rather, you really only have to be good at one thing.

In chapter 3 we will use the metaphor of lifting weights to help you gain the necessary skills to pay attention to details, listen to others, and complete projects.

Intimate relationships and parenting can often become intense struggles for adults with ADD. Chapter 4 will offer some guidance on these issues. Guidance will include inspiration and activities to help ADD adults find mystery—and therefore vitality—in committed relationships and gain skills for navigating intimacy.

Chapter 5 will reframe the typical ADD symptoms of impulsiveness, focusing difficulty, and noncompliant behavior as creativity. For example, the ADD tendencies toward being "spacey" and daydreaming will be shown to promote fortuitous insight, imagination, daring originality, and intuition.

Nature can provide adults with ADD the calming influence they need. In chapter 6 we will explore vivid case studies that show the importance of connecting to nature. This chapter will also provide reassurance and positive validation for those who fear their constant need for activity and unquenchable desire to connect with nature are simply distractions rather than personal needs and style.

Chapter 7 will review the interpersonal gifts of adults diagnosed with ADD. This chapter will also provide guidance for translating inappropriate or impulsive behavior into productive contributions. Activities will be provided for channeling the interpersonal gifts of ADD in socially skilled ways to enhance relationships.

In chapter 8 we will reframe the ADD symptom of hyperactivity as a surplus of energy. You will be guided to view your surplus energy as a valuable resource. This chapter also includes awareness exercises for appreciating your energy, and action strategies for channeling your energy.

Chapter 9 will help you understand your lack of emotional control as a capacity for emotional sensitivity and expression. Specific exercises will teach you both self-soothing techniques and how to appreciate the value of clear and intense emotional experiences.

And finally, in chapter 10 we will review the pitfalls that many adults with ADD fall into. We will also explore the promise of ADD through the successful transformation of a client who applied the principles in this book.

It's time to direct your abundant energy toward your personal transformation. I'm excited for you—you're embarking on a journey that can turn your life around!

PART 1

Getting Ready to Rumble

CHAPTER 1

"Is It Just Me or Is the Whole World ADD?"

Go for it. And while you're at it, stop and smell the roses. This is the mixed message of our culture. The problem is, stopping and smelling the roses can be a thorny business for ADD adults. I have ADD and I can't play Candyland with my kids because I can't sit still for a game meant to stimulate the mind of a four-year-old. That's the curse of ADD. We love to go for it but can't turn off the very motor that is always going for it. "Fire, ready, aim." That's the credo for many who live with ADD.

ADD DOES NOT HAVE YOU

This book will both show you the gifts of your ADD and teach you how to turn off the motor. Part of the revolution is to find and focus on what you already do well and not worry so much about patching up weaknesses. The other part of the revolution is that *you* have ADD, ADD does not have you. This book will help you find the blessings in ADD and give you the power to make choices when confronted by ADD's dark side: feeling driven, distracted, and constantly derailed.

The key is *self-efficacy.* Self-efficacy is the power you have to act on your life and affect outcomes. In self-help terms, this is *intention.* In this case, living with intention means that although you recognize that your ADD is real, you choose to live a full life—and *you* set the course for what a full life means. Once you're aware of exactly how ADD limits your life, you can begin to make different choices. You can set the intention to not be ruled by your ADD, and instead allow other parts of yourself have a say in directing your life.

THE DARK SIDE OF THE GIFT

Although scientists and clinicians are still debating the best way to diagnose and treat ADD/ADHD, the disorder is recognized as a valid neurobiological condition that causes significant impairment in those whom it afflicts (American Academy of Child and Adolescent Psychiatry 2007).

As I wrote in *The Gift of ADHD* (2005), the label ADD adds insult to injury. It reminds me of a scene from the movie *Monty Python and the Holy Grail:* When the Black Knight's arm is cut off by King Arthur, he proclaims, "'tis but a scratch." Then his other arm is cut off, too. "Barely a flesh wound," he says.

The joke is his bravado in the face of one mortal wound after another. The resilience required to maintain dignity in the face of ADD labels such as "deficit," "disorder," "impairment," "irreversible brain damage," and "affliction," is no joke.

It's self-evident that a deficit disorder causes impairment. Indeed, impairment in functioning is required to diagnose ADD in an adult. What is less evident—but equally important—is that in many ways ADD is a gift. This book will focus on both giving you more choices in response to your symptoms and seeing some of those symptoms as strengths that others do not have. I don't argue with the idea that ADD is a neurobiological condition. The evidence that ADD is genetic is compelling. If so, it makes sense that our actual brain structure is involved. ADD may be hardwired into us, but it may also be adaptive and provide us with advantages others lack, particularly in our current, fast-paced, digital culture.

Diagnostic Criteria for Adult ADD

The symptoms of ADD are real and debilitating. They can be clustered into three categories:

- Difficulty concentrating
- Feeling driven by a motor
- Impulsiveness

Many ADD experts have argued that these symptoms are all caused by a failure of executive functioning (Barkley, Murphy, and Fischer 2008; Hallowell and Ratey 2005). Whereas most people have a "little general" or an "inner CEO" in them that directs, controls, and organizes their lives, people with ADD are driven instead by impulses, whims, and emotions.

Adult ADD is a relatively new phenomenon, and as such, hasn't yet made it into *The Diagnostic and Statistical Manual of Mental Disorders* (APA 2000), the formal diagnostic manual for psychologists and psychiatrists. Leading ADD experts Russell Barkley, Kevin Murphy, and Mariellen Fischer (2008, 188) have found that people with adult ADD can often be described as follows:

- Distracted easily by unimportant stimuli
- Impulsive in decision making
- As if driven by a motor and have difficulty stopping when involved in a task
- Prone to jump into a project without following directions
- Likely to forget about promises and commitments

- Likely to mix up the order and sequence of well-defined tasks

- Likely to drive their cars too fast

- Likely to struggle with paying attention in work and recreation

- Disorganized

For diagnosis, these symptoms—except, for obvious reasons, excessive speeding—must have been present before age seven. In addition, the adult must show an impairment in functioning. A diagnosis requires six of the nine symptoms.

DIAGNOSING ADD

Because most people have some of these symptoms some of the time, ADD is often misdiagnosed. Researchers and clinicians alike have noted intense complications and pressure in making a diagnosis of ADD (Diller 2006). The pressure to diagnose ADD has been described by physician Larry Diller as coinciding with when "drug companies gained permission to advertise directly to patients in the mass media" (2006, 13). Because so many people recognize symptoms of ADD in themselves, they may go to the doctor with a self-diagnosis—often a misdiagnosis.

If you think you have ADD, you'll need to be thoroughly evaluated by a psychologist or a psychiatrist to confirm the diagnosis. This evaluation should include a medical exam to rule out health problems, as well as a lengthy interview about your work and family history. A diagnosis should also involve documentation to confirm that symptoms were present before the age of seven. This could include parents' accounts or school reports from that time. If symptoms began during adulthood, they're likely to be related to other stressors, health problems, or diagnoses.

Be wary of any professional who tells you to try medications in order to confirm a diagnosis of ADD. Because they are universal performance enhancers, ADD medications can "work" for many adults who don't have ADD.

Seeing Problems as Strengths

While the gifts of ADD—which I'll discuss at length in this book—are real, so are the pitfalls. Adults with ADD have higher rates of divorce, job changes (Barkley 2000), and drug and alcohol use than the average adult population (Lamberg 2003). But the focus of this book isn't on amplifying and explaining the pitfalls of ADD. Almost every other ADD book and expert out there has comprehensively documented these pitfalls. These books reflect the very real anguish often experienced by people who go through the world driven by passions, inner promptings, and unknown biddings.

While it's important not to glamorize the gifts of ADD, an extreme focus on the problems of ADD can also take its toll. I have worked with suicidal clients driven to despair by the unrelenting punishments of an environment focused excessively, harshly, and rigidly on what they could not do, rather than on what they could do.

By focusing on the gifts of ADD, I don't mean to gloss over the problems associated with ADD; rather, I want to give you more choices in the face of these problems.

Changing Your Thinking to Change Your Life

Cognitive behavioral therapy (CBT), a widely used and very effective form of therapy, can help you change your thoughts about yourself and the life challenges you face. CBT therapists help you focus on the positive, widening your perspective to allow you to see that any challenge can also be an opportunity. That is the function of this book—it is a therapeutic reframing of the negatives of ADD as positives.

The way out of despair and shame is to find what you do well and focus on that. By building your life around strengths rather than patched-up weaknesses, you can help your greatest gifts find expression.

THE BRIGHT SIDE OF THE CURSE

Hilarious. If I had to choose one word to sum up the gifts of ADD adults, "hilarious" would be it. ADD adults are often wildly inappropriate and irreverent. They can be the funniest, most interesting people we know. While many of us struggle with shyness, people with ADD are uninhibited, the loose cannons in the crowd. Many ADD adults were once class clowns. Hilarity separates itself from run-of-the-mill funniness in its unbelievable quality. Sometimes the adventures of ADD adults—and even their serious efforts—are hilarious. For a person punching a time card, the various ways ADD adults fill up their time and nurse their creative energies are often unbelievable. We may watch and wonder, "Is this for real?"

Hilarious or Gifted: An ADD Story

A businessman with ADD is running a meeting. A colleague is poised to begin her PowerPoint presentation. He has no patience for PowerPoint presentations and asks her to just talk instead. She stammers. He asks her to just start a conversation. She does—but within minutes he has somehow derailed the discussion and is asking her, "Haven't you ever had peanut butter stuck to the top of your mouth when you were stoned?"

While this may be hilarious, it may also cause you to wonder, "Where is the gift in that?" Well, if you're Paul Orfalea, the founder of Kinko's, who happens to be the businessman of this story, the gift lies in an ability to go beyond business blabber to get straight to personal connections—an ability that helped him build Kinko's into a business he then sold for 2.4 billion dollars. He is legendary for the prowess of his business mind. While attending a dinner party to gather stories about Paul for this book, I casually chatted with some of Paul's friends. One of these friends told me that one of his good friends—a high-level executive at Starbucks—emphatically declares that Paul Orfalea is the smartest businessman he has ever met.

THE GIFTS OF ADD

Since writing *The Gift of ADHD* (2005), I have been contacted by droves of adults with ADD. I'm always struck by their energy, the apparent inappropriateness of their behavior, their resilience, their grandiose ideas, and how very flat my world looks when compared to the ones they've painted for me. These magnificent adults have tested my capacity to set limits, piqued my interest, and sparked my sense of humor in ways that I could never have imagined. I've come to see that ADD adults not only build castles in the sky, they build *many* castles in the sky—and somehow juggle all of them at the same time. This precarious, daring, amazing, and highly entertaining behavior often makes me wonder, "How do they do it?"

As people from all over the world contacted me, I began to feel like there was an underground Renaissance occurring. These adults with ADD had minds like da Vinci and Michelangelo, minds that synthesized information from many domains, minds that didn't limit these adults to a single profession or identity. These were people who had chosen not to follow trends, people who had chosen instead to march to the beat of their own drum, seemingly indifferent to the approval—or lack thereof—of others.

Find and Focus on Your Strengths

From what I can determine, the successful CEO types in this bunch rose to their success through a combination of powerful emotional and intuitive skills and using their "hyperactivity" to overcome difficulties with organization and attending to details. Highly successful ADD adults have found ways to translate ADD's emotional sensitivity and impulsiveness into emotional intelligence, intuition, and boundless energy.

Just as type-A executives risk heart attacks and dying of stress unless they learn the basic skills of relaxation, so too do ADD executives risk failure unless they learn the basic skills of completing tasks and organization. In both cases, mastering these new skills requires discipline and training. As an adult with ADD, it's important to not only honor your whims, passions, and intuition, but also to train your capacity for attention. Sometimes this only comes with great effort and struggle.

A Japanese proverb tells us, "All vision and no action is a dream, while all action and no vision is a nightmare." Just as physical health requires logging hours in the gym or on the trails, sustained effort is also required to build the muscles that will allow you to ground your visions. This book will not only help you find and focus on your strengths, it will also highlight key areas to develop—areas that, once strengthened through training, can fuel your success.

CULTURAL CONSIDERATIONS: A WORLD GONE ADD

For many, ever-present digital and Internet technologies offer the chance to be connected globally at any—or every—minute. This scenario may be a nightmare for some, but it can be a dream come true for a person with ADD. This explosion of stimuli and information has created a culture that may be rewarding—and thus conditioning in us—traits very similar to those that signify ADD. I'll say more about this idea later in the chapter, but for now, consider the idea that in our contemporary culture, those who have the neurobiological condition that is ADD may be poised to adapt more quickly than those who do not.

For those of us who struggle with ADD, the question remains: Is ADD a gift or a curse? It depends. It depends on how you spend your time, how you make your living, and who you primarily share your life with. If the bulk of your time is spent staring at spreadsheets and reconciling accounts and this isn't something you're passionate about, your ADD energy is likely to be a curse. If, on the other hand, you juggle lots of demands and must keep abreast of many different channels at once, your ADD energy may be a gift.

Good News for the ADD Child Now Grown Up

Global changes may create a world that is a good match for the symptoms of ADD. The world is changing so fast that the workplace of the future will bear little resemblance to the workplace of today. As Thomas Friedman, author of the groundbreaking *The World Is Flat* (2006a), said dryly on MSNBC's *Tim Russert Show,* "I don't know what parents are worried about. Raising kids today is like training them for the Olympics. The only difference is they don't know which sport they'll be playing" (2006b). The industrial revolution—which led to a culture in which a person could expect to spend a lifetime in one company or specialty—is over. We're in the digital age now, and innovation is the coin of the realm in terms of job success (Pink 2005). The buzzwords of today are inventiveness, adaptability, and creativity—the very gifts of ADD.

This is good news for the ADD child now an adult. The defiance of an ADD child can transform into self-reliance as an adult, leading to both new ways of looking at the world and new solutions to old problems. An ADD child's impulsiveness can also be a great asset for an adult—particularly for those adults who have to synthesize information from many different disciplines and apply what they know in the real world. Similarly, an ADD child's hyperactivity can translate into the high energy required to keep up with a constant influx of information and ever-changing technologies. Even the low tolerance for boredom that got the ADD child into trouble in school can be useful as an adult—a perpetual quest for excitement can keep an adult on the leading edge of the ever-changing digital world. In fact, ADD adults may be perfectly suited to succeed in the culture emerging from technological innovation and globalization.

WHO YOU ARE IS ENOUGH

For an adult with ADD, the key to success is to find the courage to be who you are. This means shaping your life to fit your impulsiveness, distractibility, high energy, and need for stimulation. Don't change yourself to fit a world that others have created; rather, create your own world to be the perfect match for your strengths and weaknesses.

For example, ADD people often have too many interests to fit easily into a narrow job. When you can't find a job description that fits who you are, create your own job. A theme we will return to throughout the book is that what initially appears to be a distraction will often end up being an essential component to creating your own path.

EXPLOSION OF ADULT ADD

There's recently been an explosion of diagnosis of ADD in adults. Current estimates show that approximately four million adults have been diagnosed with ADD (Kessler, 2006). Watching a popular TV show on investing, I wasn't at all surprised to learn that sharp financial analysts are now picking pharmaceutical companies that sell ADD medications as excellent investments, citing both the growing rates of ADD diagnosis and the Drug Enforcement Agency's categorization of ADD medications as highly addictive. In this analysis, pharmaceutical companies are creating a market with their advertising and a dependency with their product; as a result, demand is likely to increase exponentially, making for a great financial investment. I'll say more in a moment about the pros and cons of medication for adults with ADD, but there is no doubt that these analysts are onto a trend.

Interestingly, psychologists and other health care professionals aren't making similar arguments. Indeed, some are dismissing the claims of an explosion of diagnosis, notwithstanding the dramatic increase in pharmaceutical sales to treat ADD for adults. The question remains: Why are so many adults being diagnosed and treated for ADD? (Remember, as of yet, there is no formal diagnostic category for adult ADD in *The Diagnostic and Statistical Manual of Mental Disorders.*)

One reason for the increase is that, as rates of diagnosis in children increase, many parents recognize similar symptoms in themselves and seek diagnosis and treatment. Anecdotally, many adults who have found their way to diagnosis through their kids have told me that they were able to get through school in their day because teachers were willing to let them proceed without too much fuss. There is a concern that the pressure to raise scores on standardized tests has made today's school system overly rigid, and in doing so, made school much more difficult for kids with ADD. Many parents think that in previous eras the demands of school weren't as crippling as they are now. This may explain, in part, these late diagnoses of ADD. Anecdotally, some prescribing doctors have observed that treating a parent can dramatically impact a child's ADD symptoms. This may make doctors more likely to urge parents of ADD children to seek diagnosis themselves.

THE ROLE AND EFFECT OF MEDICATION IN THE TREATMENT OF ADD

So, if you're an adult diagnosed with ADD, should you take medication to treat it? There's no easy answer to this question.

The research is absolutely clear: in both children and adults, medication can be highly effective in reducing ADD symptoms. I have witnessed startling transformations in ADD adults treated with medication. I've seen adults go from emotional to clear and focused, from scatterbrains to controlled forces to be reckoned with.

However, these dramatic transformations raise deep philosophical and psychological questions. I have observed that, in some cases, as individuals became less eccentric and began to conform more to societal values, they gave up various passions. For example, on medication they might spend less time and energy on causes such as political activism or caring for animals. In many cases, the people around these individuals were glad to see them give up unusual interests.

I find some of these changes disturbing. It is impressive to see a person transformed by medication, to see a person become like another—indeed a different—person. What is worrisome is that as these individuals become more like other people, they also seem to become less like themselves. In short, I wonder whether fitting societal expectations and ideals more neatly is necessarily an improvement. Depending on their level of ambition, people with unconventional interests and odd yearnings can be anything from endearing oddballs to unstoppable visionaries. Just as the perfectly apt phrase can be a cliché, so too can perfect social conformity be dehumanizing. To have the ring of being an original, something typically has to be "a little off." The deeper philosophical questions that lie behind medications reach toward the very definition of what it means to be human; the resolution of these philosophical questions is far beyond the scope of this book.

Of course, these philosophical musings don't in any way deny the mounds of data proving the effectiveness of stimulant medications in treating ADD. The fact that people go to criminal lengths to obtain these medications is also powerful proof of their effectiveness—and their addictiveness. It's ironic that the most focused, disciplined and brightest minds on the planet have spent millions, probably tens of millions of dollars, to prove what any thug on the street or Ivy League student during finals' week could tell you: Ritalin (methylphenidate) and Adderall (amphetamine/dextroamphetamine) are "good stuff." This is similar to studying whether alcohol could be helpful in alleviating anxiety. Of course individuals in a study like this would benefit. Effect sizes would be large. So it is with using stimulants.

Most experts agree that ADD medications are universal performance enhancers—anyone should expect to receive benefits from taking them. Many try the medications, see that they work, and feel certain that they must then have ADD. This may explain, in part, the increase in adult ADD diagnosis, as both doctors and patients may think like this. However, the argument that stimulant medications have specific effects for people with ADD is debatable, with conflicting evidence on both sides (Moynihan and Cassels 2002). Regardless, this strategy of seeing if the medication "works" is confounded by the medication's power as a universal performance enhancer.

The effectiveness of these medications also needs to be taken into account when considering the exponential increase in diagnosis of ADD in adults. Because these medications improve performance across the board, not just for individuals with ADD, it's possible that people may seek diagnosis simply to get the medications.

To me, it seems deeply hypocritical that the use of steroids in professional baseball has led to a national outcry and congressional hearings, while a lifelong regimen of habit-forming stimulants is being prescribed—without any public protest—for over four million adults and four million children (Diller 2006).

Where Have All the Gifts Gone?

Another concern with regard to medication is that highly effective medications may derail people from following careers or callings well-suited to dreamy adults with high needs for stimulation.

Others have echoed this concern. Jeff Zaslow, a journalist for the *Wall Street Journal,* told me that his editor wonders if medicating individuals with ADD would lead to fewer journalists in the younger generations as journalists tend to have ADD qualities. A journalist is a person who each week, with each new feature, becomes an expert in some completely new arena, connecting with sources in very different fields and tracking down leads with unrelenting curiosity. Many typical ADD traits lend themselves to the mental flexibility and lack of structure required by journalism.

If ADD meds allow individuals with ADD to embrace other, more disciplined professions, will that lead to a gaping hole in investigative journalism?

In *The Gift of ADHD* (2005), I similarly pondered the effect that medicating children with ADHD might have on environmentalism. Both kids and adults with ADD tend to be drawn to nature, to feel organically connected to it. Indeed, research confirms that nature can alleviate ADD symptoms (Taylor, Kno, and Sullivan 2001). In chapter 6, Damon Harper reports that his intense interest in preservation of beaches and other natural settings is lessened while on ADD medications.

So, although research attests to the fact that medications can indeed work, we can't ignore the potential impact of medicating ADD. While this theory is highly speculative, the gifts of ADD may include a style of consciousness that organically seeks to preserve natural resources. This connection to nature may provide the seeds of hope for staving off widespread environmental destruction; if so, medicating ADD could be disastrous for us all.

CAN TECHNOLOGY CREATE ADD?

In millions of homes, restaurants, and gathering places across the world, a husband and father is present but unreachable. He is gathering information on his BlackBerry, taking a call on his phone, or sending a text message. He is at the table but his attention is on the technologies that keep him available, nonstop, to the various demands on his time. In many families both parents are so absorbed. As a result, all of the members of the family experience an attention deficit—a lack of each other's full attention.

The recent explosion of technology and global connections has created a world where it's easy to stay "plugged-in" around the clock. The question is, what does being plugged-in do to you? Research has found that high levels of TV viewing predict ADD in children; some wonder, then, whether there might not be a relationship between the proliferation of new technologies and the increased rates of ADD in adults and children (Diller 2006). Could wireless handheld devices, iPods, cell phones, and so on actually be creating an ADD audience? The new world allows us to have instant and constant access to a steady stream of incoming information and entertainment from around the globe, quite literally in the palm of our hand. Is this technology creating a demand in us for constant stimulation? Could the powerful attractor of increasingly sophisticated and easily accessible information and entertainment be responsible for making an entire culture ADD?

The primary symptom of ADD is being "easily distracted by extraneous stimuli." Technology's lure of more answers to more questions can easily make it difficult to both follow through on other projects and organize your time and effort. What household hasn't been overturned by a family member spending hours, days, weeks, researching a medical or legal condition on the Internet? For the inquisitive mind, every medical condition, every medication, and every screening procedure is fair game for days of intensive research.

Add to this difficulty in stopping activities when necessary just two more symptoms—perhaps difficulty sustaining attention and difficulty sequencing and prioritizing—and a technophile will meet most of the basic criteria for an ADD diagnosis. If the individual's family life and other performance demands are compromised by these symptoms (that is, if the individual suffers impairment in functioning as a result), then all of the basics required for a diagnosis will be present. It's easy to see, then, how new technologies can create ADD-like symptoms, causing adults to think they have ADD. However, true ADD is likely to be genetically hardwired; thus, if new technologies are indeed increasing the rates of diagnosis, this must be, at least in part, due to misdiagnosis.

It remains to be determined how these cultural factors and technological innovations will impact an individual's long-term capacity to pay attention, stay focused, and complete high-priority projects.

REASONS FOR THE INCREASE IN DIAGNOSIS

To sum up, some plausible reasons for the explosion of diagnosis of ADD in adults include the following:

- Parents of ADD children recognize similar symptoms in themselves.
- Effective medications that are universal performance enhancers cause adults to seek a diagnosis to obtain desirable medications.
- Global and technological innovations create an ADD audience or increase in misdiagnosis.

ACTIVITY: I AM MORE THAN MY ADD

This activity is about truly recognizing that although you have ADD, your ADD doesn't have you. Simply fill in the blanks below. Even though this may feel repetitious, the more you can elaborate your identity beyond ADD, the more perspective you will gain—and the more choices you'll open up for yourself. Remember that you have a completely separate personality, with wishes, dreams, and quirks all your own, and although this personality interacts with your ADD, it isn't completely controlled by it.

Fill in the blanks:

1. I have ADD and _____

2. I have ADD and _____

3. I have ADD and _____

4. I have ADD and _____

5. I have ADD and _____

6. I have ADD and _____

7. I have ADD and _____

8. I have ADD and _____

9. I have ADD and _____

10. I have ADD and _____

After completing this activity, you may want to write in your journal about how your other roles and personality traits can help you cope with your ADD. Remember, it's important to both translate your symptoms into gifts and give yourself choices beyond just saying, "Oops, my ADD made me do it again." If you find this difficult, don't worry—the rest of this book will guide you toward giving yourself more choices.

CHAPTER 2

Find Your Sweet Spot

Now that you're an adult, you have unlimited options as to how to spend your time and energy. You can spend time with people who are like you, or with people who compensate for your weaknesses. You can work at a job that demands that you pay close attention to details, or one that doesn't. You can embrace hobbies that release your energy and feed your interests, or hobbies that challenge you to use your weaker abilities. As an adult, you have many more choices than you did as a kid. There are many different playing fields; you get to choose which ones to spend your time on.

YOU DON'T HAVE TO GO TO SCHOOL ANYMORE

If you're an ADD adult with bad memories of your school days, be encouraged: Many experts now agree that the current education system is itself outdated and doesn't prepare students for the globally connected world we now live in. Instead, the school system still prepares kids for the work life of the industrial revolution era. In 2006, *Time Magazine* did a cover story on the failings of the current education system (Wallis and Steptoe); it started with the joke that

Rip van Winkle went to sleep for a hundred years and woke up today. The only thing he recognized was the classrooms.

In part because of lack of resources and in part because of the focus on standardized measures of success, the education system hasn't moved to accommodate the dazzling technological advances of the digital age. ADD traits are a poor match for this outdated educational system. While mainstream teaching philosophy has expanded into alternate teaching techniques catering to individual styles, these developments are being put into place only recently, and with budget cutbacks these sophisticated approaches may not be applied in many settings across the country even now. And unfortunately, as many parents and psychologists report, even in classrooms led by teachers skilled in accommodating the entire spectrum of learning styles, students with ADD typically don't thrive. The good news is, you don't have to go to school anymore. The bad news is, as a result of childhood difficulties, you may have come to think that the problem resides solely in you rather than in your environment. As a result, you may be trying to force yourself to adapt to an environment that just doesn't work for you.

Indeed, trying to fit in rather than finding and focusing on your strengths may have become a way of life for you. The best way for you to embrace the gifts of your ADD is to reconsider this whole notion. Stop trying to patch up your weaknesses. Give yourself permission to jump into any arena that is a great match for your interests, needs, and skills. If you do, your entire life will change.

Sometimes the fitting-in strategy is so ingrained that it takes many small steps to even get close to embracing your strengths. If you're professionally very far afield from your real gifts, you may want to start by making your greatest strengths hobbies. Stay where you are now, but start to bring your passions into your life in small ways. Then begin to integrate your personal style into your current work life. You might start by choosing content arenas in your field that stimulate you. For example, one person who had trained to be a lawyer decided to focus on criminal law because its high drama and intensity kept her engaged and fed her high energy.

If you're trapped in the "life is like grade school" model, try to take one step away from that belief every day. A step could be anything from realizing that you can change professions to exploring a new activity you're passionate about; from becoming an artist to creating a schedule that better fits your need to mix things up. For many people with ADD, simply breaking free from the nine-to-five mold can provide a lot of relief—even when they continue to do the same job and work the same number of hours. A flexible working schedule can be an easy way to reduce the tedium of the "same old, same old."

ACTIVITY: PASSIONATE POSSIBILITIES

In this activity you will generate some specific, small steps you can take to bring passion and purpose into your life. Simply fill in the blanks below to get started.

I will do an Internet search on

[Space left intentionally blank in the original book]

I will look for adult education classes on

[Space left intentionally blank in the original book]

I will visit the local

[Space left intentionally blank in the original book]

I will call a travel agent about

[Space left intentionally blank in the original book]

I will call one person who can help me to

[Space left intentionally blank in the original book]

I will ask three friends to each link me to a useful contact so I can

[Space left intentionally blank in the original book]

This weekend I will clear my schedule so I can

[Space left intentionally blank in the original book]

Instead of watching TV, one night each week I will

[Space left intentionally blank in the original book]

I will ask a friend to go with me to

[Space left intentionally blank in the original book]

I will visit the library and find a book on

[Space left intentionally blank in the original book]

I will look through the newspaper or online postings for

[Space left intentionally blank in the original book]

When you have filled in all of the blanks, read through your answers. Is there a theme? Something that keeps coming up? If so, you're starting to narrow in on where your passion meets your purpose. Do one thing right now and schedule several of the other activities.

FIND YOUR GENIUS AND BECOME A STRONG ADVOCATE FOR IT

Another throwback to your school days is the idea that you have to be good at everything. In school, you had to make a good showing in every class, whether it be math or social studies. In the real world, you can avoid what doesn't interest you by choosing a profession in which these subjects or skills are either irrelevant or can be delegated. In fact, if you strive for balance in too many different arenas in your life, you may neglect your unique genius. Find your genius and become a strong advocate for it.

You may be relieved to know that the fundamental skill of grade school—learning a set piece of information and being able to repeat it back—has minimal value in most professional settings. In fact, many of us have had to speak to a manager about an employee who was following a rule to the letter of the law with complete disregard for the exigencies of the situation. Not long ago, I was driving to Oakland for a training seminar days after a local freeway collapse that had made the national news. I called an administrator to let her know that as a result I would be fifteen minutes late. She insisted that, although she was aware of the freeway problem, I would not receive continuing education credit for my attendance if I was fifteen minutes late. I was fortunate to find a manager in the organization who was able to consider the context and practice flexibility. In today's world, "the right answer" considers multiple competing realities and can adapt to context.

You may also be relieved to learn that the very same quality that got you in trouble in grade school—questioning the rules and considering when they don't fit—is often a central skill of those who rise to power in professional settings. Asking questions about real-world relevance and promoting flexibility in situations with extenuating circumstances are what the world needs now.

Finding the Right Match: Firefighters

It's important to remember that there are many arenas in which ADD adults thrive. Examples include journalism, emergency work, nature conservation, design, and the entertainment industry, among many others. Another great match for an ADD adult is a job that requires lots of physical activity, such as firefighting.

After reading *The Gift of ADHD* in his search to understand his motivations and talents, Captain

Scott Ohlrich of Palatine, Illinois, contacted me for further guidance. Interestingly, he noted that he, and many of the firefighters in his crew, all had ADD symptoms, but none of them had been diagnosed. This makes perfect sense: if someone with ADD finds the perfect environmental match—or what I like to call a "sweet spot"—there will be little or no impairment in functioning, the first requirement for any diagnosis, and the likely reason someone would consult a therapist in the first place.

The case of firefighters underlines an important point: Symptoms do not make a disorder. Impairment makes a disorder. If you can find your way to the perfect job for your skills, needs, desires, and, yes, even your ADD symptoms, you won't be impaired and therefore won't be diagnosed.

Captain Ohlrich described his crew to me, unwittingly mapping the symptoms and gifts of ADD onto the job requirements and general personality type of firefighters:

1. **We are emotionally sensitive:** Whether an emergency is real or only perceived, we want to jump in to help others, not just gawk at the spectacle of an event as the general public typically does.

2. **We are passionate:** Firefighters are passionate about *everything!* Ask us about the last big fire we were on, our most memorable call, our kids, or what we had for lunch—you're guaranteed to hear an interesting and lively story.

3. **We are exuberant:.** Ask anybody you know who has a friend who is a firefighter, and I'll bet they'll describe the firefighter as the "life of the party!" (You should work with a roomful of these guys!)

4. **We have unusual problem-solving skills:.** On every call, we enter an environment for which we know only a few of the necessary details. We always expect that we will be able to reach a safe and effective solution—and we do, often in less than ten minutes!

5. **We love nature:** We run, bike, climb, sail, kayak, hunt, and fish much more than your average office staff. Besides, who but a guy who really loved nature could stand on the roof of a burning house in an icy rainstorm and laugh at how he has "the greatest job in the world"?

Captain Ohlrich's story is also a touching account of how the gifts of ADD can be put to lifesaving service. How could a person take such incredible risks, deal with so many unknowns, be able to make decisions without reams of data, and yet get a kick out of standing on the roof of a burning house in an icy rainstorm unless he was impulsive, creative, and ready to take risks, and had lots of physical and mental energy to spare? Can you imagine what an adult with these characteristics would feel like sitting in an office? He would probably be literally bouncing off the walls. These firefighters probably bounced off the walls when they had to sit through school. Can you imagine a typical grade-grubbing student who only wants to know "What's on the test on Thursday?" coping with the real-life demands of firefighting? By this account then, each of us has at least some of the gifts of ADD to thank for our very safety and protection. Many of the characteristics Captain Ohlrich describes may also apply to other frontline, life-and-death professionals, including, among others, police officers, ER doctors, and EMT workers.

WHERE DO YOU FIT IN?

Instead of asking yourself, "What's wrong with me?" begin to ask, "Where would I *really* fit in?" To make the most of your ADD gifts, you have to situate yourself in an environment that is a good match for you.

Rewriting the script of your life can be hard; still, give yourself permission to think about different possibilities. Keep these in mind, and as opportunities present themselves, you may find yourself able to make unexpected choices. Steve Prevett, whom you'll meet in chapter 4, was offered management of any department he wanted in a global corporation—and instead proposed starting a virtual business within the corporation. He knew that managing lots of people and working within rigid confines would tax his needs for constant stimulation, flexibility, and creativity. And so instead, with only four employees, Steve created a virtual business that turned over twenty million dollars a year.

Steve's example underlines how important it is to take your needs seriously. As a person with ADD, you have to be realistic: following directions, adhering to a rigid schedule, and having little flexibility will drive you nuts. If you have the opportunity to create a work experience that will match your needs, don't hesitate—negotiate for it. In Steve's case, he was offered an opportunity that most people work their whole lives for. He turned it down, creating instead a challenge that was a perfect match for his gifts, work style, and needs.

Rather than blame yourself for not fitting into a rigid environment, seek ways to create your sweet spot—an environment that matches your needs. Creating a sweet spot typically requires you to advocate for yourself. Use your knowledge of your gifts to negotiate for whatever you need in order to bring your innovation, high energy, and creativity into the workplace.

An excellent resource for helping you find your sweet spot is my book *Listening to Depression: How Understanding Your Pain Can Heal Your Life* (2006). Depression can be your body's way of telling you that you are out of your sweet spot; this book contains many activities to help you discover where your passion meets your purpose. The simplest way to get some quick answers is to explore the following questions adapted from *Listening to Depression* (2006, 65):

- What would be too good to be true? (Dream big—imagine something that previously seemed unimaginable or far outside your comfort zone.)

- If your life were to get easier and easier and better and better over the next six months, what would you be doing six months from now?

- If you knew you could not fail, what would you do with your life?

One powerful lesson I've learned from working with people is that very often the only thing separating you from your dream is a limiting belief. Once, when I was on a radio show, a man called in and said he would love to work in a pet store because he loved animals and thought it would be fun. Getting a job would be easy and the pay would be the same. Why didn't he do it? He believed it wasn't manly to work in a pet store, and so instead slogged away at a job that didn't spark his soul. I worked with him to see through his limiting belief that real men don't work in pet stores. Although my contact with him ended with the radio show, by the end of the call he seemed to be headed toward his sweet spot.

Whistle While You Work

If making changes in your work environment itself is too big of a leap for you right now, you can still start to shape your world by bringing your gifts into the workplace. Start by taking seriously the primary needs of ADD:

- To be constantly stimulated
- To feel excitement
- To change your pace often
- To be able to innovate
- To create structure rather than follow others

Addressing a specific need can be as simple as listening to punk music on your iPod while doing administrative work; or leaving your office to meet with people rather than sending an email or picking up the phone; or maybe suggesting fun activities to coworkers, or spearheading charity walks. Do whatever it takes to give yourself a sense that you're shaping your work life, not just being shaped by it.

ACTIVITY: MEET YOUR NEEDS

It's important to make a major mental shift and translate your symptoms into needs that you can honor. Give yourself permission to be who you are.

1. Below is a list of qualities or elements that adults with ADD typically need. Circle all that apply to you:

Excitement

Physical activity

Constant stimulation

Innovation

Inventiveness

The opportunity to mix it up

Flexibility

Creativity

The ability to create structure rather than follow directions

The ability to space out

Frequent breaks

Self-determination

Access to natural world

2. Write down five more needs that are related to your distractibility, hyperactivity, and impulsiveness:

[Space left intentionally blank in the original book]

3. Take out your journal and begin to explore how you might honor these needs at work. Try a few ideas out. Start small and observe the effects on your feelings and performance. Keep a detailed log of what increases productivity and what doesn't—this information can be very useful when you negotiate for changes in your work environment.

BUILDING STRENGTHS RATHER THAN PATCHING UP WEAKNESSES

When you were a child, your life may have revolved around identifying your weaknesses and patching them up. As an adult, it's a whole different ball game. As an adult, not only can you situate yourself in an environment that matches your strengths, you can also choose to focus on finding and growing your strengths rather than your weaknesses.

Of course you will still have to address weaknesses, but in the right measure. Constantly analyzing weaknesses, where they came from, and how you can cover them up or work on them should be a thing of the past. In his extensive research on marriage, John Gottman discovered that happy marriages have a ratio of five positive interactions to one negative interaction (Gottman et al. 2002). Adopt this same ratio in your relationship with yourself. For every weakness you patch up, go out of your way to identify five strengths. Give yourself credit for what you're doing right. Build on strengths you've already identified. You can even make a game out of it and keep a tally in a notebook or on a dry erase board at home or at work.

For example, if one of your weaknesses is that you fail to double-check your work and as a result often overlook careless mistakes, you'll want to address this weakness. If you also set in motion the counterbalancing force of finding and focusing on five strengths, your motivation to address your weakness will increase. (Alternatively, in some situations you may find yourself rethinking whether or not this "weakness" really needs to be addressed at all.) For example, in this case, you might have these five strengths:

- I save time by doing a good-enough job.
- I'm more forgiving of others' mistakes.
- My ideas are original.
- I have the enthusiasm to get others to sign onto a project.
- I can use my sense of humor to put it in perspective.

Try this yourself—list one weakness and five strengths below:

Weakness

1. ______

Strengths

1. _____

2. _____

3. _____

4. _____

5. _____

If you consistently find that in your current workplace, at home, or in other settings you're focusing on patching up your weaknesses rather than building on your strengths, you should probably start looking for a different environment.

Appreciate Yourself

Shifting your focus from weaknesses to strengths may require a revolution not just in your way of thinking, but in the way you have lived your life thus far. Make a commitment to actively search for your strengths. When you find one, articulate it to yourself. For example, if you navigate a difficult situation with grace, tell yourself, "That was tough, but you pulled it off." Make a practice of constant appreciation. If you find this difficult, choose an appreciative catch-phrase and simply commit to saying it ten times a day for a week.

Examples of general appreciative catchphrases include:

- I like how I did that.
- I handled that well.
- Great job!
- If I keep at it, the sky's the limit.
- This is tough, but I can handle it.
- I can bounce back.
- I'm really gaining momentum.

Even if it feels forced, commit to saying one or more of these statements to yourself ten times a day. This will naturally cause you to identify opportunities to appreciate yourself. Even if you keep your commitment simply by saying a catchphrase apropos of nothing, you'll still feel better and begin to find subtle ways in which the catchphrase is actually true. The power of creating a self-fulfilling prophesy cannot be overstated.

In addition to using a catchphrase, appreciate yourself by changing the questions you ask yourself to focus on your strengths. Start with the following two questions:

- What am I doing right?
- What's working in my life?

Your answers will naturally boost your mood by directing your attention to your strengths. However, the really radical element of this approach lies in what you can do with your answers: create a life that revolves almost entirely around what already works and what you already do well.

CHANGING EXPECTATIONS: FROM CONVENTIONAL ACHIEVEMENT TO CREATIVE CONTRIBUTION

With their natural creativity, ADD adults are poised to set the world on fire. Thus, if you aim only for technical perfection in a field and restrain your ability to be a pioneer in whatever you do, you may sell yourself short. For children, excellence is typically defined as either mastery of knowledge others have deemed necessary or perfection of techniques modeled for you. As an adult, standards change; to be truly excellent you must become a creator of knowledge. You must find your unique angle—your unique gifts—and bring it to whatever you do.

As an adult, excellence, or greatness, means that you don't just follow standards laid out for you by someone else, you define new standards. Fundamentally, you get to define what success means. Many people define success as getting the most goodies (money, status, promotions) by following directions better than everyone else or working harder and longer. ADD adults often fall miserably short in this particular rat race. But there are other pathways to greatness. One such path is to figure out what comes easily for you—what you are exceptionally good at—and then build on these gifts.

Even something like an inability to follow directions can be turned into an asset. Observe yourself and see what you are doing differently from others. Write down and record how you are doing things—what you say differently from others, how you listen and respond differently from others. These differences may be signs of innovation rather than defiance. Explore these differences—these are areas where you can become a pioneer.

Similarly, you can use feelings of shame or of being different to help you discover where your creative contributions lie. If you feel ashamed or embarrassed about some difference, follow this feeling to its source. Elaborate this difference precisely: how do you act differently, feel differently, think differently, or see the world differently? The answers to these questions may contain the very seeds of a creative contribution that will make a huge difference in the world.

In my own life, I struggled with my clinical training because I didn't see clients the way other psychologists did. (I still resist talking about clients in the detached, objective, clinical way that other treatment providers do; personally, I find this insulting.) It always seemed to me that clients had good reasons for their pain; beneath bad behavior often lay a poignant, heartbreaking reality. Other care providers would gloss over the harsh realities an individual faced, focusing instead on clinical labels. No one paid much attention to the positive qualities of clients—qualities that were usually glaringly obvious to me. I found myself questioning every diagnosis and doubting the life sentences that came in the form of prognoses. For a while I wondered why, and this difference made me intensely uncomfortable. I have since been able to translate this difference into an approach that focuses on strengths and finding meaning in symptoms.

There are surely many such areas in your life, too, where you just don't jibe with the mainstream view of your field or area of interest. Instead of wondering what's wrong with you for seeing things differently, observe and record the nuances of your perspective and points of contention. Remember that creative contribution and originality don't come from a mainstream view; by its very definition, innovation requires that something be startlingly different from what is already accepted by others.

WHY THE WORLD NEEDS ADD ADULTS

The theory of natural selection outlines how random genetic mutations can offer members of a species certain advantages—particularly when living conditions change. Consider your ADD as a genetic, hardwired condition that may similarly offer many advantages today. What are the defining features of the new world, and what qualities do ADD adults have that might offer a good match?

Unrelenting Curiosity

An individual who succeeds in today's economy will have a greater chance of success if she is intensely curious. Many businesses and corporations now require employees to interact with cultures all over the world. The more interested you are in learning about the cultures you interact with, the greater your chances of success. Also, the ability to synthesize information is becoming increasingly important at many different job levels. The greater your capacity for exploring different domains and broaching arenas of knowledge outside of your specialization, the greater your chances of success.

As a child, this very same curiosity may have gotten you into trouble. Teachers may have viewed your questions as defiant, or blamed you for derailing the class in your pursuit of the unknown. Thankfully, not all teachers are this way. Personally, I've always found that the curiosity and unrelenting questions of ADD students have expanded my thinking. Regardless, the ability to consider questions that we don't have answers to is a true gift, and it can lead to amazing unexpected discoveries.

Who Says?

ADD students often get into trouble for taking the stance "who says?" And yet, no ability is going to be more sought after and important in the information age than this one. On the one hand, there is a tremendous amount of good information easily accessible on the Internet. (A huge boon to people who have difficulty memorizing information or holding on to minute details!) On the other hand, there is a lot of bad information on the Internet. As we come to rely more and more on the Internet, it's going to become exceptionally important to question the sources of online information.

I'm often surprised by the information that my clients pull off the Internet. Living in the San Francisco Bay Area and being a fan of self-improvement workshops, I'm pretty open-minded about alternative approaches. However, even I am often shocked by treatment suggestions clients have found on the Internet.

What concerns me isn't the wackiness of these suggestions but the fact that some of the information from online sources is downright misleading; sometimes it can even derail a person from other approaches that truly will help. For example, one TV celebrity demonstrated her treatment of choice for depression: hanging upside down in a contraption. There are many effective approaches to healing depression; pursuing a misleading approach like this one can prevent people from getting the help they really need.

In this digital information era, it's important not just to take the information we find with a grain of salt, but to actively question its source. Curiosity, the insistent demand to push the boundaries of what is known, and asking, "Who says?" are exactly what the world needs right now.

Leadership and Innovation

As a person with ADD, you're probably more interested in shaping your environment than being shaped by it. This is a fundamental characteristic of ADD; it's often labeled "defiance" or sometimes "inability to follow directions." (In the profile that follows, Bill Jacobs Jr. calls this quality "manipulation," but manipulation in the good sense of the word.) It means you want to impact or change the world you live in. Outside of the classroom this is called leadership. If you can effectively tap into your desire to change the way the world operates, you will go far in your professional career.

For example, many of my ADD clients not only want to solve their own problems, they want to change how I conduct their therapy sessions. Sometimes this takes the form of telling me about new technologies that I could use for my phone consultations; other times they tell me how I should proceed in therapy. Indeed, many ADD clients come to me with specific approaches they would like to use. If it falls within my areas of competence I'm happy to try out whatever they suggest.

In the workplace, this is called innovation. In the current culture—and most industries—innovation is the only way to survive and thrive. Being at the head of a technological curve and doing things better and more quickly can help businesses get ahead. This is true even if you aren't in the technology industry itself—the adoption of cutting-edge technologies drives most industries.

When you begin to recognize your own gifts, you set the stage for real-world success. The following is a profile of one adult with ADD who was, by his own account, a failure in school, and yet achieved happiness and great success by doing what he loved and embracing his differences as unusual and distinct abilities.

Bill Jacobs Jr.: ADD Means Not Paying Attention to What You're Not Interested In

Bill Jacobs Jr. owns eight car dealerships that bring in over four hundred million dollars in sales every year. He barely graduated from high school and never made it through college. He is, in fact, a classic example of a successful adult with ADD. As he describes it, the very same traits that impaired him in the classroom cause him to be highly sought after as a board member by many of the nation's leading corporations.

Given his stature as a businessman, I was surprised by how easy Bill was to talk to; our conversation was fluid and informal. Bill was remarkably open about his successes and struggles. As a child, his was a textbook case of ADD. Today, two of his own sons have been diagnosed with ADD. He did poorly in school, never doing much—if any—work. Although he went to college, due to his poor performance, after two years he wasn't asked back.

Our conversation took place in June 2007 over a series of phone calls sandwiched between his busy schedule and my busy schedule. From what I could gather from the changing background noise during our multiple conversations, he seemed to be moving in and out of various ongoing activities. It seemed a conversation only two ADD people could have—often derailed but also filled with insights, inspirations, and even revelations.

Gift of Adult ADD Number One: Taking Visions Seriously

Bill's dedication to taking visions seriously and using them to create positive change was a constant throughout our discussion. Bill spearheaded the Rush Neurobehavioral Center in Chicago, a nationally recognized treatment center for kids with learning disabilities. This organization was born when Bill mentioned to his son's psychologist his frustrations at having to take his son to appointments with specialists spread all across the city. In response she described her vision of a single resource center for parents and children where psychologists, psychiatrists, neuropsychologists, and other treatment providers could all be centrally located. He took that vision and helped make it happen, creating a yearly fund-raising event that raises over one million dollars each year to support the center.

From Classroom to Boardroom

Bill can take in information from diverse sources, filter it through multiple channels, and offer compact summaries of the processes and content of possible solutions. I observed this myself in our interview—despite frequent breaks between our conversations, he always seemed to anticipate the next turn of conversation and yet be able to bring us back to the fundamental point at hand.

When Bill was a child, this ability to take in information from many channels led to problems in the classroom. Teachers wanted him to focus on only one channel and regurgitate material back to them to demonstrate his powers of attention. However, this "symptom" of firing on multiple channels, which left him bored, distracted, and disruptive in the classroom, led to excellence in the boardroom.

In the boardroom, business leaders want comprehensive solutions to complex problems, solutions that both honor existing realities and open up new vistas of possibility. Individuals with ADD can often fulfill this need more effectively than highly focused individuals. A highly focused individual can be derailed by the minutiae of information found on a single channel, and can miss many of the complexities involved in real-world problems. On the other hand, the ADD capacity to juggle and explore various ideas at once can lead to breakthrough analyses and syntheses.

Interestingly, Bill succeeded at a time when businesses all around him were failing. He succeeded in part because while these other businesses closed down, he expanded his business, buying even more dealerships. This daring approach, due in part to his rejection of trends and his preferences for multitasking and manipulating his environment, led to the scale of his success today. These qualities—challenging the climate, going against the grain, and embracing many opportunities rather than focusing on just one—are all related to his ADD.

At one point, I tried to egg Bill into saying that his ADD style of multitasking and taking on multiple deals was actually the linchpin of his success: "If you hadn't taken on multiple leveraged buyouts while others were going out of business—if you had instead stayed focused on running one dealership—maybe you would have been one of those that didn't make it." His response was clear and direct: "No. No matter what I'd done, I would still have created the success I have now."

It would have made a nice story, this idea of not concentrating in one arena as the saving grace. But he offered me a better story: His diamond-hard confidence that, regardless of his decision to take on multiple deals, his abilities, his intuition, and his energy would have led him to where he is now. The understanding that ADD is a gift offers great resources in itself. While the symptom of multitasking was helpful, it was Bill's ability to feel in his bones the advantages his ADD offered that was in part responsible for his huge success. The better story is this: Once you understand that ADD is a gift—that it makes you different from others, and that this difference will help you get ahead in the real world—you cannot be stopped.

Finding His Sweet Spot

Bill attributes much of his success simply to working in the arena of cars. Cars are something he is passionate about, even obsessed with. Professionally, his businesses sell cars; personally, he collects cars. His personal cars range from a 1936 Bentley to a 1952 Ferrari Barchetta. He likes to take his cars out, sometimes for four-day rallies. When I asked Bill what would have happened if he'd ended up in some arena other than cars, Bill was almost stupefied by the idea of taking a path that wasn't the one he loved. He replied, "I could never have done anything else. I couldn't have taken it for even a minute." Perhaps, then, for Bill, the fundamental gift of his ADD may be the inability to do something he didn't feel absolutely driven to do. Perhaps other people can choose paths for other reasons, but for many ADD folks, living outside of the sweet spot is unbearable.

Bill elaborated on this theme, "I wouldn't let myself get into any arena other than cars—cars are my passion. You can go so much farther if you follow your passion. I can't deal with boredom, I can't tolerate things I don't like."

His comments led me to an epiphany: ADD means you can't pay attention to what you're not interested in. Why are we so convinced this is a terrible deficit? Its opposite—focusing all of your attention on your passions—is a wonderful gift and can lead you to a life of fulfillment.

Emotional Intensity

The telltale ADD symptom of emotional intensity—which can get ADD kids in trouble but play out spectacularly well in adults—shows up in Bill as devotion to his wife and four sons. His conversation is almost entirely taken up with his delight in his sons. Two of his sons have been formally diagnosed with ADHD, the other two have not.

A vexing familial concern, obviously at the forefront of his mind, surfaced three or four times during our discussion. Bill said, "My wife says to me, 'Why can't you even look like you're listening when we are out for dinner with another couple?' I don't know why, but when I'm at a social situation like that it looks like I'm not fully present, when I actually am listening."

I asked him, "Could you be present in a way that others don't easily recognize? Perhaps you're intensely present but not listening to the exact words spoken. Perhaps you're instead getting a feel for who everyone is at the table, absorbing the ideas discussed, and moving in your mind far beyond this particular discussion, while still staying deeply connected to it. Is it something like that?"

It was. Bill added, "I am in demand as a board member exactly because others see that even though I may be doodling or look like I'm not paying attention, in the end I can tie it all together and offer a plausible plan of action that entirely accounts for the multiple demands and possible pitfalls that others have raised. They can see by my results that I have been there the whole time, taking everything in at a high level."

Considering again his social dilemma, I imagined Bill at a dinner table, trying to fit his brilliant, wide-ranging, high-speed, multiple-channel mind into friendly banter of interest to two couples, all the while constrained by social niceties. He didn't describe this, but the scene that played itself out in my mind is a common one for individuals with ADD.

Bill took his wife's complaint very seriously. Indeed, the seriousness with which he considered his predicament spoke of his devotion to his wife and his earnest wish to figure out, once and for all, how to address her frustrations with his way of listening.

While struggling with this dilemma, he spoke of seeing a similar characteristic in his oldest son, diagnosed with ADHD at the age of six: "He had a teacher who made him take notes. He never learned anything when forced into that mold. When he was allowed to just listen, he got everything. He would look totally disconnected, but he could repeat back every word the teacher said. If teachers were willing to adapt to his style and look beyond the fact that he didn't look involved, he would do well in his classes."

In reflecting on his son, Bill revealed how close he himself had come to becoming discouraged by his own experiences as a child and made some interesting points about both the social consequences of our current school system and the importance of giving children with ADD a shot: "For me, when I received negative feedback in school early on, it was sometimes hard for me not to turn off. Did you know that 60 to 70 percent of inmates in this country have learning issues? This is a serious matter. They just turn off when no one can appreciate what they have. But kids who learn in alternative ways can be much more successful in business than Harvard-trained book-worms because they can navigate systems. If children with ADD can get one break, one opportunity in the right situation, they can succeed."

From Bucking the System to Charming the System

One word that emerged over and over again in our conversation was "manipulation," used in a positive way. Jointly we defined it as a key feature and gift of ADD. Whereas many people scan an environment looking for relevant rules to follow, a person with ADD doesn't react to what an environment already is, but instead tries to actively shape it. During his two years at Colorado State University, Bill took a logic class but didn't do any work for it. On the final he explained—in perfect logician's terms—why he shouldn't be flunked. He got a D. For Bill this story is an example of how the gifts of ADD (in this case, charm and cleverness at manipulating environments) can remedy some of its deficits or learning differences.

I asked Bill what had turned it all around for him, what had enabled him to move beyond the lack of confidence he often felt at school as a child. He told me, "Once I started accomplishing things, my motivation kicked in. The more I did, the more recognition I got in the world, the more I saw I *could* do. I began to see that I have a special thing, a heightened awareness, that others do not have. This snowballed when I saw that in the real world I had as much or more talent than others. The more I took on, the more I got done—I could get deals done that no one else could. For kids with ADD today, if you get one opportunity, one chance to shine, you can turn it around."

Bill's final comments hit home. One chance. One opportunity. If parents, teachers, and psychologists can show these kids what they can do, lives can be saved and sweet spots found. What if Bill had been turned off by all the negative feedback he received as a child? When self-esteem is lost, a person's gifts to the rest of the world are often lost, too. Bill Jacobs Jr. played a pivotal role in starting one of the nation's most respected treatment centers for children with learning disorders. Because he believed in a vision, innovative programs are now being developed and researched. Each year at the Rush Neurobehavioral Center, 1,500 families are given a different message than the one touted by the deficit-disorder model that tells us that this constellation of traits is a fundamental flaw. Thus, through Bill, the most essential trait of ADD adults—chasing dreams—has led to concrete, profound differences in the lives of thousands of kids and their families. This is the sort of gift that can get lost when we focus on what's wrong instead of what's right.

CHAPTER 3

In the Workplace: Now Patch Up Weaknesses

Because the workplace often evokes memories of school, many adults with ADD bring wounded feelings to work every day. Over the many interviews I conducted, I was struck by the fact that no matter how successful a person was, the pain of school days was still raw when recalled. Many people with ADD have memories of mean-spirited comments being regularly directed toward them during their childhood; often adults with ADD carry the scars from these into the workplace.

Some ADD adults adapt to the work world by allowing themselves to be pitifully underemployed. Rather than find a great match for their skills and interests, they will work at a job far below their natural abilities. In this way, their inevitable screwups and difficulties with following directions will be balanced by being more capable than those they work with. This strategy has its own set of painful problems. For one thing, knowing you could do and be more can lead to an enduring agony. For another, you may find yourself falling prey to negative feedback from people who aren't as smart as you are.

Another strategy ADD adults sometimes adopt is to overcompensate, working inhuman hours to try to avoid possible criticism. It can be shattering when even this strategy doesn't prevent criticism from heading your way, whether from colleagues, bosses, or clients. Another problem with this strategy is that it can take a tremendous toll on your personal relationships.

Some ADD adults bring their great gifts to bear in arenas that are good matches but, like someone driving with one foot perpetually on the brakes, they never go anywhere because they are drinking, using drugs, or struggling with some other addiction. This outcome can be heartbreaking for your family and friends. Not only are they aware of your shining gifts, they must also bear witness to the destruction of these gifts. Unlike the strategies of playing small or working tirelessly, in this case your great gifts are present for everyone to see—as is the loss of these gifts through your self-destructive habits.

The tragedy of these three work-life compromises (playing small, workaholism, and destructive habits) is one and the same: an utter loss of self-worth, caused by an environment that focused only on what a person couldn't do well and hardly at all on what the person *could* do well. The losses—both in quality of life and to the communities that desperately need the contributions of gifted ADD adults—can be mammoth in scope. For example, when a disgruntled office worker who could be a brilliant artist doesn't receive the validation and support necessary to pursue her art, not only is she unhappy, but her community has lost an artist, a businesswoman, and a leader.

Whether it be from overburdened teachers, exasperated family members, or friends, ADD adults often enter the workforce with some mean-spirited internal voices telling them they are doomed to fail. These messages may include some of the following:

- You'll never amount to anything.
- You're a mess.
- You disrupt everyone wherever you go.
- You'll never learn to follow directions.
- You're lazy and stupid.

These are just the tip of the iceberg. Many ADD adults have internalized negative messages that no one actually ever said to them. They may have started saying harsh things to themselves after constantly experiencing trouble and unrelenting failure. These beliefs can cause more trouble than the ADD itself.

ACTIVITY: CREATING A NEW REALITY

To silence these internal messages and allow yourself to heal, write out any messages that you either hear yourself saying or remember others saying to you, and then transform them:

1. In your journal, write down the specific hurtful words people have said to you. Also, write down anything you say to yourself that brings you down.

2. Once you've done this, find a way to turn these messages around. Write an affirmation that addresses the belief. (These affirmations don't need to feel true yet.) Affirmations should focus on recognizing the strengths of who you are rather than on a need to change the underlying DD. or example, you may believe "No matter how hard I try, I can't do anything right." In this case, while it's good to say, "I can achieve anything if I work hard enough," it's even better to say one of the following affirmations that will also honor your personal style:

- I am loving being a huge success while working in my own style at what I love.

• I am loving achieving my dreams and offering great service while taking it easy.

• I am loving effortlessly making all my dreams come true.

Start affirmations with the stem "I am loving" to decrease any inner resistance. Sometimes if you state an affirmation straightforwardly, such as "I am effortlessly making all my dreams come true," another part of your mind says, "No way, life has to be hard," thereby counteracting the affirmation. By saying, "I am loving effortlessly making all my dreams come true," there is nothing to resist—almost everyone would agree that if you do indeed make your dreams come true effortlessly, you will love it.

BUILDING YOUR ATTENTION-TO-DETAILS MUSCLES

In the previous chapter, I suggested maintaining a roughly five-to-one ratio of focusing on gifts to patching up weaknesses. It is important, though, to remember the one in that five-to-one ratio. Let's take a look at how to improve a common area of weakness for ADD adults: paying attention to detail.

Adults with ADD can be terribly careless. Difficulty paying attention means that we often miss details. Carelessness can take the form of having to pay late fees every month because you don't get your bill in on time or ruining a project because you missed an essential detail.

There is no way around this issue. ADD is a deficit and a disorder. Carelessness is one of the defining features of an attention deficit. Attention to detail isn't a task that you can delegate to someone else, and every situation in life requires attention to detail. It is a weakness you must set out to improve.

Strengthening your capacity to pay attention is like weight lifting: If you want to gain muscle strength, you have to work consistently and frequently. To build muscle you have to commit to both going to the gym and monitoring your diet—and not just for one day, week, or month, but for the long haul. So it is with building your capacity to pay attention. It's hard work and requires consistent effort, but if you apply yourself you will see positive results.

You may feel discouraged that something that comes so easily to others will take time and effort for you. Consider this: The typical profile of an ADD adult includes a weakness in attention to details and a strength in creativity. It is far easier to train yourself to pay attention to details than to train yourself to be creative. And creativity comes much more easily for you than it does for a person who is extremely focused on details. Each of us has a profile of weaknesses and strengths.

Valuing Details

One reason ADD adults often overlook details is because they are more interested in highly stimulating, big ideas. A constant need for stimulation makes slowing down to review work—work you're probably now very familiar with—feel like torture. In order to build your attention-to-detail muscles, you have to first understand the value of details.

You probably feel that creating something new is more important than going over or perfecting something that is old. In short, new is stimulating and old is boring; attention to details means spending time with material that is "old." You may also justify skipping details because you're gaining time by not double-checking your work. However, your ability to slow down and pay attention to details is what's known as a universal ability, meaning that it applies to everything, including what you love or care about. If you have a unique perspective to share with the world but mess up major details when you try to explain it, you may fail to get your message across.

If you care about sharing your ideas, it may help to just face reality and realize that packaging can be everything. If you want your ideas and projects to have impact, the details have to be right. Find within yourself a core desire that will motivate you to pay attention to details—something that's bigger and broader than getting approving nods from others, something that's in alignment with your guiding vision or sense of purpose.

For me, an emblematic moment of the importance of paying attention to details was getting a C on an English paper. When I asked my English teacher why the paper had been given this grade, she told me it was actually the best paper in the class but I had stapled the pages together out of order, some of them upside down. It had taken her twenty minutes to unstaple the pages, figure out the correct order, and put them all back together again. Thus the mediocre grade for what was, by her account, an outstanding paper.

Quick Tips

In addition to tapping into the motivational force of your core desire, use the following quick tips to help you pay attention to details. These easy techniques can help you get the job done when the stakes are high.

Start Small Set aside five minutes at a time to pay attention to details. As with weight lifting, small efforts accumulate when you do them regularly. Besides, it's easier to motivate yourself to pay attention to details for five minutes than to face a gargantuan job, knowing you have to examine it thoroughly and carefully.

Mix It Up Pay attention to details for five minutes with full concentration. Then, for your next five-minute set, go to a coffee shop. Or put on some music. If your detail check involves something that you can print out, get up and walk and review for five minutes. If you were sitting at a desk, sit on the floor.

Redefine the Task Find different ways to think about tasks that require you to pay attention to details. For example, see a task as improving efficiency rather than checking details. How can you review a chunk of material faster than you previously have? Having a problem to solve will make a task more interesting.

Create a Paying-Attention-to-Details Nook Create a special area dedicated to paying attention to details, an area so inviting that you don't mind spending long periods of time in it. This could be as simple as throwing some pillows on the floor and letting yourself sprawl out. Decorate, post heartwarming photos, play soft music, use scents—do whatever you can to create a comfortable place to pay attention to those pesky details. If the nook is inviting and comfortable enough, you won't mind the time you spend there. Also, it will serve as a trigger, helping you to slide into a mind-set of focused attention more easily. If your work setting doesn't give you a private office, save some of your work to take home and create your nook there.

BUILDING YOUR LISTENING-TO-OTHERS MUSCLES

You can't follow directions unless you've heard them in the first place. Not listening to others is major deficit that can wreak havoc in a workplace. As I wrote in *The Gift of ADHD* (2005) not listening is a gift gone wrong. ADD adults typically have a hard time listening to another's words even when deeply attuned to the other person. The reason for this is that in conversation, people with ADD often use their intuition and emotional sensitivity to get a feel for who the other person is and what the other person's emotions, intentions, and motivations are at that moment. For example, you may not hear the specific instructions your boss gives you because his voice is so monotonous that you start to wonder if he is repressing something, an idea which then distracts you further. Interestingly, your assessment of your boss may be right on; regardless, missing his instructions will impair your work performance. This is a dilemma

ADD adults often find themselves in. It reminds me of Emerson's quote, "Who you are speaks so loudly that I cannot hear what you are saying."

Intuitive empathy can be a great gift because it gives you information other people tend to miss or just skip over. But in the workplace, where you often need to acquire and retain specific information in order to do your job, this can be a problem. Unfortunately, paying attention to the specific content of another person's words can sometimes be painfully difficult for an adult with ADD. When working on this skill, think again of the metaphor of weight lifting: this, too, is a skill to build slowly over time through frequent, regular practice.

Valuing Listening

When learning to listen to the words other people are saying, finding and focusing on your core desires can help motivate you. If your heart is invested in a larger mission, recognize that poor follow-through due to not listening may dilute your message. Indeed, just one person not listening can ruin rare opportunities. For example, when a scientific researcher who was conducting a study on responses to a certain event—responses that were not replicable—hired an assistant who didn't listen to directions, the assistant introduced a serious flaw into the data collection, preventing clear conclusions from being drawn. When you are tempted to tune out, think of what's at stake. Even if your core desire is as straightforward as keeping your job, try to put it front and center. Also, review times when your failure to listen created problems for you. Consider how you could have done things differently and develop a plan for moving forward with greater commitment to listening.

As an adult with ADD, one of the main reasons your mind wanders when listening to others is that your need for constant stimulation easily causes you to feel bored. When you are bored, you tune out. Trying to find something more stimulating to focus on, your mind roams. This, too, is a reflection of the gift of your lively and curious mind. You get bored easily when others speak in carefully modulated voices, their words focused solely on passing on information. You're stimulated by emotions and connection—a distant voice that is just reciting information rather than trying to connect with you makes is hard for you to focus on the words spoken.

One of the other reasons you get bored easily is that you typically grasp overall concepts very quickly. While you may skip over details, you generally understand both main ideas and where a person is coming from very quickly. People without ADD often repeat or circle around ideas they are trying to convey when they sense that an individual with ADD isn't fully paying attention. Such repetition can be very irritating; your own irritation can then distract you further.

You may also space out while others are speaking as a result of the gift of your emotional intelligence. If you sense a discrepancy between what the person is saying and her inner emotional state, you may doubt your connection to the person—and tune out. You may also "catch" whatever emotion you sense the other person is feeling. For example, if the person talking to you is angry but trying to appear calm, because of your emotional sensitivity you may actually begin to feel her anger. This flood of impinging emotions can confuse you and distract you from the words actually being said.

And finally, you may have difficulty listening to others because you fire on multiple channels. This is like multitasking but applies to your thinking and feeling. You have channels both for different aspects of the same information and for entirely different content areas, and you process all these elements at the same time. A person giving you a straightforward set of instructions will only take up one channel—leaving your other channels itching to be used. What other people see as your distraction can be simply your need to occupy multiple channels at the same time.

Quick Tips

The following are some quick tricks to help you listen to the words of others, even when you feel like bouncing off the walls.

Breathe If deep breathing can get a woman through giving birth, it can get you through droned instructions. Keep your mind focused on the words of the other person while deliberately taking slow breaths. If you want, you can use a specific breathing pattern, such as a four-second inhale through your nose followed by a four-second exhale through your mouth. This will calm you down, at the same time increasing your ability to focus. The effort to consciously breathe will take up one of your channels, thus meeting your need to multitask.

Connect Drifting Thoughts to Actual Content Find ways to connect your mental distractions to what the person is actually saying. This can be fun, as many times it takes creativity to find connections between the two streams of incoming information. Interestingly, this is a central strategy used by therapists to understand clients at a deeper level. Many therapists believe that their distracted fantasies, thoughts, images, and emotions are directly related to the person talking or what the person is talking about. You may find this to be true in surprising ways.

Be a Roving Reporter Pretend that you're an investigative journalist—imagine you'll have to go back and write a story on what the person is telling you. This will help focus your attention on details and keep your mind occupied. Like a reporter, get the information you need by asking who, what, when, where, and why. These questions will help you gather the details necessary to fully follow directions and put a plan into action.

Put Emotions on a Shelf When you can't listen because you're distracted by your sensitivity to the other person's emotions or your own intense emotion, imagine putting this emotion temporarily on a high shelf. Tell yourself that you can return to this intruding emotion after you have gathered the information you need. If more emotions emerge, put them on your imaginary shelf, too. If a stream of emotions comes, put each of the various emotions in an imaginary box and then stack them all on the shelf. Promise yourself that you will return to explore these emotions after you have gathered the information you need.

Feel Sorry for the Other Person Gain the motivation to listen to people who irritate you by feeling sorry for them. If you're frustrated by how slowly people talk, how they repeat information you already understand, or how overly constrained and uptight they are, feel sorry for them that they're highly stressed and consumed by work demands. You might also feel sorry for them for losing perspective or being unable to loosen up. Once, a person I was supervising who had difficulty listening to me blurted out, "You need a beer." Of course it was inappropriate, but I laughed and admitted I was indeed feeling tense at that moment. His comment, reflecting his attunement to my inner tension, allowed us to connect and then move forward at a more relaxed pace. However, you don't need to share why you feel sorry for the other person—sometimes it will definitely be better not to! Just switching in your own mind from irritation to compassion should do the trick.

Repeat Words Back Challenge yourself to find key phrases or words to repeat back to the person talking. Active listening like this requires you to paraphrase what the other has already said. For example, "You were really frustrated when Sheila didn't come through for you." This is another task that can change a situation's context, forcing you to listen to the actual words spoken. If you make a game of it, listening to the other person will become a challenge, and hence more interesting. Initially, you may find this difficult to do for long periods of time. Again, remember the metaphor of weight lifting: each time you repeat back a thought or phrase, consider it a repetition in the weight room. You are not only gathering necessary information, you are also building your listening-to-others muscles.

LEARN TO BOUNCE BACK

One of the best ways to tackle arenas where you are flailing around with little success is to learn how to relate to failure. If you find yourself in a setting that isn't a good match for you, you may feel like a failure. Similarly, if you have failed in the past in settings that were out of sync with who you are, you may be too paralyzed by fear of failure to move on. Two steps can help you move on. The first step is to let yourself feel the disappointment fully. Even if your worn-out dreams weren't a good match, they still were very real dreams. You may need to grieve in order to begin the process of letting go of outdated dreams of who you are and what you want. The second step is to buck up and bounce back—show the world and yourself your resilience.

Each time you fail but bounce back, you build strength and resilience. Having greater strength and resilience will allow you to persevere longer than others who have not experienced failure. Having greater strength and resilience will also prime you for success by making you immune to the minor and major setbacks that may derail others. As Paul Orfalea, Kinko's founder, has wisely observed, failure actually means one or more of three things (2007, 126):

1. You're a risk taker and (within reason) that's a good thing—you know how to take initiative;

2. You've learned something about yourself or the world along the way; and

3. There is another, probably better, opportunity elsewhere.

Begin to translate your own disappointments into these three "gifts" of failure. For example, ask yourself:

1. How did I show boldness or take a calculated risk, and how can that serve me in the future?

2. What skills or lessons did I learn from this failure?

3. If there is a better opportunity for me, what might it be?

Brainstorm these questions, writing down any free associations. It's important to remember that if you take a risk and fail, that doesn't mean that taking the risk was wrong. By definition, a risk includes a substantial chance of failure. In fact, many risks lead to failure—if this weren't the case, they wouldn't be risks! Don't beat yourself up if a risk leads to failure. While you may not know what opportunities await you around the corner, assume that they are there. Let your imagination run freely.

Failure Can Become Freedom

Fear of failure impairs many people, keeping them stuck in small lives because they are afraid of breaking their streak of straight As or constant state of approving nods from their environment. The best way to get over any fear is exposure therapy—in this case, being exposed enough to failure to realize that it doesn't have to stop you. Losing your fear of failure can be very freeing. When you lose your fear of failure, you gain the power to experiment in life and work, and experimentation leads to innovation and discovery. Thus, the capacity to take risks without undue fear of failure is directly related to creativity and discovery.

If you haven't lived up to your own—or others'—expectations in school, relationships, or work settings, it is important to address these failures with both positive thinking and negative thinking. What do I mean by negative thinking? I mean examining closely what went wrong and what you could do differently in the future to achieve a better outcome. For example, if you observe weeds in your garden, practicing positive thinking and repeating, "There are no weeds; there are no weeds," isn't going to be much help. Rather, you need to recognize the weeds and set about uprooting them. Similarly, if you haven't lived up to your expectations, identify any underlying problems and work on solving them. Problem areas for adults with ADD are fairly predictable. The following are some common reasons that adults with ADD fail:

- Not listening to others
- Not following directions
- Not paying attention to details
- Disruptive behavior
- Unreliable behavior or performance

These are just some places to start looking for your "weeds." After you have identified the root cause of your failure, either strengthen your relevant weakness or change your circumstances so you won't have to contend with it so. For example, you might choose to work for yourself rather than an employer, or you may seek greater alignment with your passions.

Finally, after you have honored the path of negative thinking, it is essential to move forward with the full gusto of positive thinking. Remind yourself that, within reason, there is no path that is closed off to you, not if it's in alignment with your greatest passions and strengths. Remember, too, that failure can serve to bring you into better alignment with your greatest gifts and passions. When you face failure, you have at least two choices: you can believe that this failure gives you important guidance, or that it means you are impaired in some way. Ask yourself, "Which of these beliefs will be more helpful for moving forward?" You don't need to wonder which is really true—each can become true as a self-fulfilling prophecy. Choose to believe that a failure offers you important guidance and seek to understand what exactly that guidance is.

This is one of the great gifts of ADD: it forces us to find our sweet spot. Whereas others, because of their discipline and follow-through, may be able to do well in arenas far removed from their greatest gifts, ADD adults are often forced by failure to find what they love.

Paul Orfalea, the founder of Kinko's, has both ADD and dyslexia. He ran his business entirely around his strengths, hardly bothering to build up his weaknesses. Paul now teaches at the University of California, Santa Barbara (UCSB). The Orfalea Business Seminar, taught within the global and international studies major, guides students to real-world applications of business in a global environment.

Paul Orfalea: ADD as a Learning Opportunity

Paul Orfalea was diagnosed with ADD and dyslexia as a child. He describes himself as always being at the bottom of the class, and remembers being punished heartily for not following directions or learning assigned material. He was able to get into the undergraduate business program at the University of Southern California by taking satellite courses and forging connections with professors. He graduated at the bottom of his class, with straight Ds. He reports, however, that he only aimed for Ds, as he knew from an early age that he would run his own business and thus wouldn't need to impress anyone else with his credentials. And indeed, he went on to start Kinko's, which he developed into a global corporation and then sold for 2.4 billion dollars (Orfalea, 2007, 176).

A simple interview couldn't begin to contain who Paul is and what he does. As is to be expected between two adults with ADD, our discussion was unfocused. I met with Paul in Santa Barbara, California, in June 2007. I completely failed to gather some of the information that I would have liked to gather. But both Paul's personal style and the way the interview unfolded are emblematic of ADD.

When you look into Paul's eyes, you have the distinct sense you're looking at a genius. On the one hand, his genius lies in his remarkable ability to bring new things into the world. But he is a genius, too, in the sense that psychologist James Hillman uses the term in his "acorn theory" (Hillman 1996). Hillman writes that every single person has a gift; however, this gift may be beaten out of us by conformity and control by others. Hillman suggests that a person becomes a genius to the extent that she stays in alignment with her greatest gifts.

In Paul's case, he understood his ADD as a gift and stayed in alignment with it rather than fighting it. In his memoir *Copy This! How I Turned Dyslexia, ADHD, and 100 Square Feet into a Company Called Kinko's* (2007), Paul writes that he succeeded in founding Kinko's *because* he had ADD, not in spite of it. In his book, Paul tells of being so hyper that he was unable to sit in his office. As a result, he began to wander around the stores where he worked. By seeing what was going on in his stores—and getting actual, real-time experience—he was able to create a company that catered precisely to the needs of its clients.

One of Paul's mantras is "You don't have to be good at everything; you just have to be really good at something." This is consistent with James Hillman's acorn theory, that our whole development can be understood in terms of who we will become. Hillman argues that what happens in your childhood may be essential for the development of the genius that you are meant to be. This was certainly true for Paul.

During our interview, Paul mentioned that he hadn't worried about being punished in school, because he'd known he would run a huge company someday. He casually recounted a story of being punished in third grade for refusing to learn how to write. During his punishment, he told himself, "I will never need to know how to write; my secretaries will do it. I'm going to run my own business." His confidence in this vision of someday running his own business—a business he knew was going to be big—kept him from focusing on the message that he was incapable that he was getting from those around him.

Paul talks very casually about always knowing clearly what he would do in the future. While not typical or articulated in the literature, one of the discoveries of my research and interviews with adults with ADD is that such experiences of clear knowledge may be related to the symptoms of ADD. In the next chapter, you'll meet Steve Prevett. He similarly described having such clear, precise images of the future that he learned to overcome any obstacle in order to make the future he saw happen. Perhaps ADD adults fail in school and at work because these intensely clear visions of the future give them a strong sense of what they need to know and what they don't. While it may look like they're failing on a day-to-day basis, they actually have a brighter future in mind and hence know they don't need to pay attention to things that others tell them are important.

If Paul knew that what he was learning in school wasn't relevant to what he would do in the future, his lack of attention can be seen as simply reflecting an accurate perception of what was important to his own life. It opens up the possibility that when ADD kids complain that school isn't relevant to the rest of their lives, they may be right.

I soon came to realize that Paul Orfalea exists on a completely different playing field from anyone I had ever met. He is entirely driven by his curiosity, whims, and interpersonal intuition. He wasn't at all concerned about social niceties, social norms, or the fact that our meeting was an information-gathering interview.

Read Me Like a Book

One of Paul's gifts is a strong interpersonal intuition. For example, at one point during the interview I became preoccupied by a personal concern. It was only for a few minutes, because I soon realized that Paul had started talking about preoccupied women. Paul had, in fact, taken the conversation to a place that perfectly mirrored my inner experience; this is what I mean by interpersonal intuition. ADD adults often read the inner experience of others moment by moment, changing the content of their conversation to reflect these perceptions. This is why their conversations often seem derailed and tangential.

Paul, though seemingly off topic, was actually perfectly present in the moment: I was distracted and preoccupied and, as a result, his conversation became about distraction and preoccupation. He didn't point his finger at me and say, "You're preoccupied," but it was clear from the way his conversation followed the reality of the moment that he was reading me like a book.

Emotional Sensitivity

Paul's life demonstrates both the gift and the peril of emotional sensitivity. On the one hand, his pain was obvious in talking about the heartaches of school. He repeatedly spoke of how much he had hated school, how irrelevant school had been for him. On the other hand, his intense sensitivity also compelled him to pay close attention to the needs of his employees; as a result, Kinko's was often one of *Fortune Magazine*'s top one hundred places to work.

Paul expressed heartache at the way his employees were treated by "the Wall Street suits" after he gave up control of the company. Paul repeated over and over again, "They didn't care; they didn't care." His anger was intense as he talked about how he "couldn't believe what they did to Kinko's."

When I asked him what had been the worst of it, he erupted, pain clearly evident, "They fired all of these people, all of these people lost their jobs. Do you know how many people depend on you when you run a business? And all these people lost their jobs because of them." At this point he hopped out of his seat and ran away. My heart sank. I didn't know where he had gone—or if he was even coming back.

He returned within a minute, twenty or so coffee stirrers in his hand. Selecting one, he broke it apart, put part of in his mouth, and started chewing. "This is what helps me, this is what people with ADD need to do, this really helps me to maintain my energy," he said, chewing on the coffee stirrer. It was clear that even many years after he had left Kinko's he still cared deeply about those who had worked for him.

ADD and Global Culture

During our conversation, there was only one moment that resembled a typical information-gathering interview. Somewhere in the middle of the frenetic free association and the nerve-jangling flow of emotions and ideas, he asked me, "Are you getting what you need?"

His question was the opening for me to bring up a question he was perfectly situated to answer: "Well, I've been thinking that in some ways an ADD adult is ideally suited to the current business climate, given its emphasis on globalization, innovation, and access to digital technologies. What do you think about that?"

Paul said simply that he agreed with this idea. Five seconds of silence went by.

I tried again: "I was hoping you would say more since you have so much experience—with Kinko's you built a global business that in many ways catered to this new ADD culture and now you teach in the UCSB global business program."

He answered, "Well, you shop. You know as much as I do."

Dead silence.

If he were a Zen master and I his student, this would have been the moment of enlightenment. Instead, I sat stupefied, my mind stopped in its tracks by this incomprehensible puzzle.

Paul continued, "Women make better investors than men..." Another tangent.

It was only later, in reflection, that I took in the depth and power of his comment. A person who shops knows as much about the global economy and business culture as a man who built, from scratch, a global business that earns two billion dollars a year—a man, moreover, who teaches a global business program at UCSB.

Was Paul crazy or was he onto something? Later, I asked a student of his, Brian Rocha, what he thought. He thought Paul's point was brilliant: "Business is driven by demand. Analysts make mistakes when they forget that it's all about the customer. Businesses succeed when they remember this and meet this demand. He's right."

Whether Paul's judgment is right or wrong, his respect for customers comes not from logical business analysis, but rather from a gut instinct and generosity that are part and parcel of his ADD.

Hilarious

Paul Orfalea is an outspoken advocate for lactation rights and facilities, a fact that struck me as humorous. As a mother who worked while nursing children, I'm serious about this issue, but that a global business tycoon should also be a strong advocate for breastfeeding rights—something that has its share of women detractors (for example, Barbara Walters)—seemed funny to me. Funny in the way of many ADD adults, class clowns whose adult pursuits and interests are often highly unpredictable and may unashamedly challenge social roles and norms.

His class-clown nature was also evident at a gathering for his global business course. Over and over again I heard students talk about his generosity, his love of teaching, his brilliance in business. It was clear that students were learning information from him that would apply to their real-world experience.

During this gathering, Paul was asked why he teaches. He replied, with great humor, "All ego." He continued, "When I was college-aged, no girls would look at me. Now, when I teach this class, pretty girls look at me all of the time." His self-deprecating humor helps to create the charisma that almost all ADD experts recognize as common to ADD adults.

Later, as I reflected on my interview with Paul, I realized that, if I had met with him just to gather biographical information, I had failed miserably. It was a delightful experience, however—one that only began to capture his lightning-quick genius.

His constant refrain is "You do not have to be good at everything like they tell you in school. You just have to be very good at one thing." These words, a comfort to any person with ADD, reflect the central theme of Paul Orfalea's life: find your passion and pursue it.

CHAPTER 4

Relationships, Parenting, and ADD

You may wonder if you'll ever be able to settle down in a relationship and you may be afraid that no one will ever just let you be yourself. You may have to tell yourself, "Listen, listen, just listen," when communicating with loved ones. You may feel tormented as you try to be patient with a partner who seems to move in slow motion compared to your own tempo. You may wonder, "Why do *I* always have to slow down? Why can't anyone try, just for one day, to keep up with *me?*" You may practice mental gymnastics trying to be present for high-quality time with significant others and children.

Part of the challenge you face in relationships is to show that your need for action and stimulation isn't a character defect, but a difference—an exciting one in our world of controlled enthusiasm. In short, to show that who you are is not a deficit disorder that has to be covered up at every turn. If you can help your partner see the world from your point of view for a while, you'll be on your way to a fulfilling relationship. This is an essential step: having to adapt to another's worldview 24/7 is a recipe for resentment.

Not being patient, not listening, and not wanting to sit still are not crimes. With these "deficits" come a lively mind and a life filled with fun and excitement. You have much to offer your friends and family simply by staying centered in your own personal style. Define yourself in your relationships as different, not disordered. If you can articulate—to yourself and others—how your ADD is a gift, it won't rob you of your vitality and life.

You won't last in a relationship in which instances of your ADD traits are always labeled as bad behavior. Having other people tell you that you aren't up to par can be extremely painful. It's simple and straightforward: when someone tells you there's something wrong with you, it hurts. To build a strong relationship, you'll need to advocate for your gifts. If your partner is demanding that you change, you may need to work on redefining your problems as strengths. Build intimacy by explaining your hurt feelings to your partner.

If, instead of doing so, you try to cover up the fact that it's hard to have someone tell you that there's something wrong with you, your hurts can lead to a general numbness that will impair your ability to connect deeply with your partner. Your partner calling you a "spaz" or saying you need to "chill" at every turn can take a serious toll. For an authentic connection, it's essential to share with your partner that you are hurt. Practice saying that you've been like this your whole life and it hurts to be told there's something wrong with who you are.

If you believe that you shouldn't feel hurt—or even worse, that you deserve your partner's complaints—you're going to want out of the relationship sometime later down the road. Being stuck in never-ending reform school is a recipe for resentment; at some level you will feel that your partner neither understands nor accepts you. This resentment, if not acknowledged, will go underground and slowly destroy the relationship. Resentment like this can fuel further impulsive behavior, making both you and your partner likely to see it incorrectly as simply a symptom of your ADD.

Because adults with ADD constantly crave new experiences, maintaining a long-term relationship can be a struggle even without this burden of steady criticism. As resentment builds, an ADD adult's need for stimulation is likely to create an irresistible impulse to find another partner. However, often partners simply don't understand ADD; if they're educated about it, they won't be so critical. The following are some sample statements you can use to advocate for yourself:

- "It's true I'm not listening, but it's because I'm attuned to your emotional state."

- "It's true that I can't sit still with the kids, but I can be lots of fun."

- "It's true I can't be as patient as I would like, but I keep our social life hopping."

These are just to give you some inspiration. The rest of the book will serve as a guide for translating "bad behavior" into simple differences or gifts. Use this guide to show your loved ones what you are doing right.

CREATIVITY

For adults with ADD, relationships are often cramped by their limited patience for many of the activities that others enjoy. Any activity that is slow in pace, requires a lot of attention to detail, or otherwise just doesn't sit well with an ADD adult can feel like torture. For obvious reasons, this can cause problems in relationships; for example, when your partner loves to play backgammon and you'd rather pluck your eyelashes out than concentrate on its rules. Or when your partner enjoys the subtleties of foreign language films and you just want to see the latest action flick. Though these problems can at times seem insoluble, their solution lies in creativity.

These examples are really only conflicts from a rigid, narrow point of view. Actually, there are a greater number of other engaging and fun activities—activities you and your partner would both enjoy—than could be finished in a lifetime. It only takes creativity to find and explore these. It may well be that you will never share your lover's enjoyment of backgammon, but if there are ten other activities that make both of you happy, who cares about backgammon? For example, if both you and your partner enjoy Italian food, there are many activities that will let you share this interest. To name just a few, you could visit different Italian restaurants, take a trip to Italy, read cookbooks, or collect Italian wines.

ACTIVITY: ONE HUNDRED WAYS TO LOVE A LOVER

There is no reason to fight with your partner about different interests. Instead, just focus your attention on interests that you share rather than those you don't.

1. First, each of you should write a list of one hundred interests. These could include intellectual topics, sporting events, activities, food types, or any broad arena that piques interest. Nothing is too lowbrow or highbrow.

2. After you have compiled your lists, review them to identify overlapping interests. Create a new list

of these overlapping interests, then rank the various items on this list together. This process of identifying overlapping interests doesn't have to be an exact science, just a general sketch will do.

3. For each shared interest, list as many different activities as you can think of. For example, if you both like gospel music, you could visit music stores, attend concerts, go on drives while listening to CDs, share downloads with each other, take singing classes, read books on favorite artists, watch TV shows of live performances, start a gospel blog, create your own greatest hits lists, or write your own gospel songs. One interest can generate many activities.

4. Go through your top five shared interests and, working together, create a list of ten activities that both of you would enjoy. Don't get bogged down in whether or not you would absolutely love the activity, just choose things that seem fun to do together.

5. Use this final list to begin planning activities. As you focus on activities that both of you enjoy, new interests will open up.

You may wonder, "But what about those activities that are a real passion for my partner but would be torturous for me?" You can demonstrate respect for something a partner is passionate about without being involved in it yourself. For example, you could give your partner a special backgammon set, a book on backgammon strategy, or a night off family duties to play backgammon with others. In this way you can demonstrate respect for your partner's passion while still honoring your own way of being in the world.

To the extent that you compromise who you are and what you want, you set a relationship up to fail. This doesn't mean that the other person is there to meet your needs. It means that you can't consistently compromise who you are to be accepted by the other person. Your ADD is part of who you are. If your disorganization, distractibility, and need for stimulation are viewed solely as problems, the relationship will struggle under the weight of judgment and resentment.

THE LISTENING GAME

At the same time as you put your foot down and insist on your ADD qualities being honored as an essential part of who you are, you should also make an effort to improve your ability to listen. The major complaint of those who are in intimate relationships with ADD adults is that they don't listen. Indeed, ADD adults are notorious for not listening. For many adults with ADD, listening to others can feel almost impossible.

In some cases, you may actually be listening but look so spaced out that others think you're on another planet. In addition to the listening techniques suggested in chapter 3, try the following experiment.

ACTIVITY: WATCH THE CLOCK AND LISTEN FOR FIVE MINUTES

Just as you built your ability to pay attention to details through five-minute practice sessions, you can also use this incremental method to increase your ability to listen. You probably have a hard time listening because you feel like conversations go on forever. As a result, you may interrupt or change the topic. However, your sense of time is distorted by your feelings of urgency and almost instant boredom, so sometimes you interrupt a person who has been talking for only a few seconds.

Do this listening experiment for only five minutes—you'll be amazed by how much the other person can get out in such a short time. And by promising yourself you'll only spend five minutes listening, you will give yourself a psychological safety valve. After listening, make sure the other person knows you were listening by repeating back the main points you heard.

1. Pick a time to try this experiment. Choose a time you usually get in trouble for not listening to someone you are in a relationship with. A good time may be when a partner gets home from work and wants to unload daily stressors. Make a commitment to try to listen to your partner for five minutes.

2. Watch the clock and do not interrupt for five minutes. If you find yourself getting distracted, immediately bring your attention back to the conversation at hand. Although you may feel like you want to hurl yourself against the walls to see how far you will bounce, remind yourself that after five minutes you can stop listening. Tell yourself this is a test of endurance.

3. At the end of the five minutes, summarize everything you remember. For example, "Wow, it sounds like you had a really hectic day. First you had a lousy commute, and then there was that awful meeting, and then Susan wanted the proposal done by the end of the day. At least you got to stop at the gym on the way home." Give yourself permission to do whatever you need to take care of yourself. That may mean you need to leave to address something else; for example, "I need to get out of the house for a while. Now that you're home, would you mind hanging out with Robbie while I

go for a run?" If you're like most ADD adults, your partner will be shocked and pleased that you have listened for a full five minutes.

When Your Partner Gets Repetitive

ADD adults can't stand it when people repeat themselves. But this repetition is actually a vicious cycle ADD adults in part create. Because of the ADD impatience and tendency to interrupt, other people feel they are not being heard—and so keep repeating themselves, which in turn makes you tune out even more. However, remembering the following simple concept can turn around all of your social conversations and even your most important relationships:

When others feel heard, they will stop repeating themselves.

From the perspective of efficiency, it's more than worth it to invest five minutes in listening and then repeat back what the other person has said. If you do so, often the whole repeated conversation will then be over. For people in long-term relationships, this can end a dysfunctional pattern that has gone on for years—perhaps even decades. People will keep saying the same thing until they feel the message has been received. Just hear it and repeat it back. When people feel heard, they will usually stop repeating themselves.

Expert BS Detector

Another reason adults with ADD tend not to listen—or at least look like they aren't listening—is because they can see when a person isn't totally in alignment with her words. You can call this phoniness "impression management" or just plain old BS; regardless, ADD people are so tuned in to what's really going on with a person that they often don't hear the person's words. Address this problem by tactfully sharing your perceptions or observations with the other person. This can be as simple as saying, "You seem stressed-out," to a person with a fake smile, or just stating your own reaction: "You're saying one thing, but your expression suggests something different."

When you use this strategy, you show the other person that you are at least tuned in on some level, even if you aren't taking in every single word. This can facilitate your connection and intimacy.

SEX IN THE ADD SITUATION

Some of the main symptoms of ADD—particularly impulsiveness and the need for constant stimulation and excitement—hold both great promise and great peril for relationships. The promise lies in the fact that, because ADD adults are impatient and bored easily, adventurous sexual activities can be highly stimulating to them, making them good lovers. The peril lies in the fact that this attraction to what is new and different can also cause ADD adults to find it difficult to stay monogamous in a committed relationship. As another factor, ADD adults are also usually uninhibited emotionally and interpersonally. This lack of inhibitions can be sexually attractive to others, thus leading to further temptations for ADD adults, who are already easily tempted.

The upside is that once an ADD adult makes a commitment, life won't be boring—the ADD adult's creativity will keep things lively, both in the bedroom and in other areas of life, such as social and recreational activities. There are many pathways by which an ADD adult is capable of making a commitment. The following is a story of how a life-changing insight helped one man settle down into monogamy.

Because ADD adults are typically very sensitive, they can be highly aware of the toll a wandering eye can take on relationships. One person I interviewed spoke of a revelation he'd had about monogamy. He'd found the woman he wanted to spend the rest of his life with. As he described it, "I wanted to be lying next to her taking naps every afternoon when I was ninety years old." He loved her, but like many individuals with significant others who won't make a commitment, she was often anxious that he was interested in other women. This constant worry tainted their relationship and put him on edge. He realized suddenly that if he made a commitment to her, she would get what she needed, her anxieties would be put to rest, and they could both finally enjoy a relationship that wasn't soured by constant worry. He realized that to get the relationship he wanted, he needed to give the woman he loved what she needed: a commitment. He realized, too, that over the course of his life he had ended multiple relationships as a result of sensing an anxious energy in the women he cared for. The fact that it was his inability to commit that was causing this anxiety came as an epiphany to him—one that led him to a happy marriage.

ACTIVITY: BACK TO THE FUTURE

Impatience and impulsivity cause many relationship problems for ADD adults. Indeed, temptations of the moment can sometimes carry more weight than long-term needs and desires. This activity will help you consider the long-term benefits of your choices.

1. Imagine you are at a party celebrating your twenty-fifth wedding anniversary. Where would your party be? Most importantly, who would be there?

What gift would you give your spouse of twenty-five years?

2. If you struggle with temptation and are currently in a relationship, is the person you are committed to the one you want to be with at your anniversary? Or do you want to be there with someone else? How will you feel, on your twenty-fifth wedding anniversary, about the person who is now triggering you to consider cheating on your partner? How would indulging your temptations make you feel on that day in the future? Would it be worth it?

3. If you feel it might be worth it, make a list of ten people you have been attracted to in the last ten years. Write down your feelings toward each of those people, and whether you acted on your feelings or not. Review this list. What can you learn from it about your feelings of sexual attraction? How can you recognize the difference between people you want in your life for the long haul and those who won't meet your long-term desires and needs? As you look over this list, what decisions do you want to make moving forward? Write about what you've learned in your journal. If you still think cheating on your partner is a good idea, you may want to seek support from a therapist to help you figure out how best to move forward. These feelings are

probably a signal that there are substantial issues to work through in your current relationship.

THE GIFT OF ADD PARENTING

Most ADD parents feel guilty because there are things they can't do well with their kids. For starters, as a parent with ADD, you may not be able to sit still long enough to play games designed for young children. While most adults have difficulty with mind-numbingly boring games, the high need for stimulation in ADD adults makes this task well nigh impossible. However, buried in this is another gift. One of the reasons for your impatience is the intensity of your experience in connecting with your child. Because your ADD grants you such emotional sensitivity, you may find both your love for your child and your child's neediness overwhelming. This sensation of being overwhelmed is often felt as impatience. Other parents may experience their child with the intensity of a slow burn rather than a blazing fire, and therefore be able to stay more patient over the long haul. Your blazing intensity is nothing to apologize for. You get drained so quickly because you are highly attuned to your child's needs.

ACTIVITY: KEEP YOURSELF ALIVE AS A PARENT

Before you blame yourself or your impatience, realize that you can fill the time you spend with your children doing activities that you enjoy. Look at the following list. Circle any of the jobs that you would actually be interested in doing. Notice that many of these jobs are part of the work of parenting. Keep yourself alive as a parent by spending more time on those tasks that you love. (Table 4.1)

sports coach	conflict mediator	stage manager
trash collector	entertainer	gardener
advisor/counselor	referee	tailor
public relations expert	Santa and Tooth Fairy	waiter/waitress
tutor	impersonator	image consultant
promoter	research and development	barber
mediator	engineer	doctor
judge	cheerleader	chef
police officer	translator	CEO
lawyer	personal shopper	handyperson
therapist	personal assistant	event planner
occupational therapist	dishwasher	medical assistant
speech therapist	professor	DJ
bath attendant	choreographer	lifeguard

masseuse	producer of plays and	preschool teacher's aide
housekeeper	musicals	neighborhood ambassador
crisis hotline volunteer	activities coordinator	waste management
teacher	chauffeur	interior designer
caterer	cleaner	art collector
organizer	nurse	museum curator
launderer	financial manager	party planner
nutritionist	accountant	travel agent
psychologist	musician	artist
hairdresser	photographer	crafts teacher
short-order cook	librarian	
secretary	documentarian	

Table 4.1

With all the roles and activities a parent has to take on, if you are prone to feeling guilty there will always be something to feed your guilt. On the other hand, realizing how many roles a parent plays can give you permission to spend most of your time on activities that intrinsically interest you.

Develop a strategy to spend as little time as possible on activities you don't like and as much time as possible on activities that you do. One strategy you can use that will work miracles is to respond to your child's request to play with, "Yes, for five minutes." By keeping an activity short, you can meet your child's needs and at the same time honor your own. Your child's attention span is short, too—when five minutes are up a child will often be satisfied enough for you to get up and attend to your own needs. Even if a child protests when the time is up, you can simply redirect him to continue playing independently. The five minutes you spend with your child in the activity (playing hide-and-seek, reading) most likely would have otherwise been spent negotiating, arguing, or disciplining the child for negative behavior. Thus, this strategy leads to a win-win situation: your child gets some playtime and you don't have to spend that time—or even more—managing your child's disappointment.

The following is a worksheet to help you keep yourself alive and honor the things you already love to do.

Do What You Love; the Kids Will Follow

Five activities you love to do with kids	Five activities you hate to do with kids
[Space left intentionally blank in the original book]	[Space left intentionally blank in the original book]
Five activities you like but don't have time for	Five activities that sound like fun but you don't do

[Space left intentionally blank in the original book]	[Space left intentionally blank in the original book]

Table 4.2

Which activity(s) can you delegate to someone else (partner, babysitter, sibling)?

How can you do something you love while doing an activity you really don't like? (*For example, create an interesting story line when playing make-believe or bring a magazine to a soccer game*)

[Space left intentionally blank in the original book]

What activity can you redefine so that it's fun for you? (*For example, instead of building train tracks, play trains by lining chairs up and sitting in a seat while the "conductor" collects tickets and drives the train.*)

[Space left intentionally blank in the original book]

How can you do something useful while doing something you don't like? (*For example, doing stretching exercises while playing a game on the floor.*)

[Space left intentionally blank in the original book]

Which activities can you limit to five minutes a day?

[Space left intentionally blank in the original book]

Which activities can you limit to ten minutes a day?

[Space left intentionally blank in the original book]

Which activities can you limit to fifteen minutes a day?

[Space left intentionally blank in the original book]

The preceding worksheet will help you practice focusing on your strengths rather than your weaknesses. The following is a profile of a successful ADD adult who attributes his happiness as a husband and a father to treating his ADD tendencies as gifts; although he has developed strategies to overcome weaknesses, he doesn't try to fit into a mold that he is not. Steve Prevett is a forty-five-year-old business owner and father of two daughters. We communicated by phone and over e-mail over the course of many months in 2007. I also spoke to his ex-wife Jeanette for two hours on the phone, and communicated via e-mail with his fiancée Helene.

Steve Prevett: Rediscovering Unrecognized Gifts
Steve's story parallels that of Paul Orfalea and Bill Jacobs Jr. in that he did poorly in school but succeeded in business in part because of his ADD traits.

"I was top gun," Steve said, describing the opportunities that opened to him after a management assessment program demonstrated that he had achieved the highest overall score on a range of tests, including mental agility, IQ, problem solving, financial ability, and interpersonal communications. Given that he'd dropped out of school at sixteen, this feat was especially meaningful for him—a vindication of sorts.

Although the global corporation he worked for offered him a senior executive position in any department he wanted, he decided to try something a little different. He decided to cater to his ADD traits rather than work against them. He didn't want to manage a huge department, didn't want to have to contend with bureaucratic machinations. So, instead, he used this opportunity to create an entirely new business within the larger corporation, a business that, despite having only four employees, went on to take in twenty million dollars a year. Then, at the height of his corporate success, he made another unusual decision—to quit and start his own business.

Steve is not only remarkable in terms of his professional and financial accomplishments, he is also remarkable for the sophistication with which he can articulate how he channeled his ADD characteristics to nurture his romantic and parenting relationships.

Relationships and Future Memories

Steve described to me a phenomenon that almost every other person profiled for this book also reported: seeing clear, convincing, filmlike clips of the future. Together, we named these visions "future memories." By Steve's account, these images of the future are so vivid that when he experiences one, he lets go of all doubt and works hard to make the future memory happen. He credits future memories with creating the companionship of both his first marriage and his current relationship.

When Steve was a teenager, he met and fell in love with Jeanette. Jeanette was initially reluctant to date him, but Steve's persistence won out. He reports having clear, immediately real images of marrying and becoming inseparable from Jeanette. These came true when, at the age of twenty-one, he married her. Similarly, although he was told by many of his family and friends that buying a house was "crazy and impossible" at the age of nineteen, he defied these commonly held expectations to do just that with Jeanette two years before getting married.

Thus, his clear visions of the future became a reality.

Although they were given, at best, only an 8 percent chance of having children, Steve's ability to precisely envision the future helped the two of them overcome these medical odds to have two daughters. On this he said, "Again I think my vision of the future played a big part for me here, as I seem to have spent a lot of my life knocking down barriers to make visions a reality. I just won't take no for an answer." For almost twenty years Steve and Jeanette lived a close, intense, happy life together. However, in their thirties he and Jeanette began to develop in different directions; by the time Steve was thirty-seven years old, their marriage was beginning to fail. Now divorced, they remain friends and active coparents of their two daughters, to whom both are devoted.

"I felt deep down that a chapter in my life had ended, as if the 'film' had," explained Steve, "but I somehow also knew that this didn't mean my life with Jeanette was void and gone forever, just entering a new phase. You can't erase such a big part of your life—it's there for a reason and makes you who you are. Also, your commitment to your kids is never ending. Still, sometimes it's hard to explain to them that your marriage is over, but not your life as a loving parent."

Although it was painful to end their marriage, Steve had a vision that both he and Jeanette would come through it okay, remaining friendly and raising their children cooperatively. (Jeanette was equally focused on a new future reality; she is now in her sixth year of training as a psychotherapist and, like Steve, also engaged to a new partner.) However, Steve realized that it would be easy to fall into the trap of living a lie—a life that your heart and soul are not in—under pressure from others. Steve's ability to envision a positive outcome for himself, Jeanette, and their children encouraged him to live a life that wasn't a lie, but was real. At the same time, this positive future memory pushed him to work hard to ensure that his relationship to Jeanette didn't simply die, but instead transcended their divorce to operate on a different level.

The same ability to precisely envision the future that led to his first marriage and their success in having children also led to his current romantic relationship. From the time Steve first met Helene, he was convinced that she was part of his future. However, he and others thought she was an unattainable partner. It seemed impossible that he would ever have a relationship with her. Yet, again he began to have compelling, filmlike future memories of time spent together and activities shared. These were so vivid and convincing that he began to believe that Helene would be a part of his life. In the early days, Helene had major concerns about entering into a long-term relationship with him, due in part to his family situation. They separated for a while. However, because he was sure it was right for them to be together, Steve persisted. Steve and Helene have now been together for five years and recently became engaged.

In many ways, Steve and Helene are opposites. She is neat and tidy, with advanced degrees in law; he is disorganized and creative, and never completed his high school education. While Helene likes order, planning, and a nine-to-five workday, Steve feels caged in by planning and prefers a flexible schedule, sometimes waking up in the middle of the night to unleash his creative business ideas. In spite of this polarity, both find that their happiness relies on being together. As Steve noted, "We're opposites, but it works. We can have a relationship; we just have to recognize our differences and accommodate them. Problems happen in relationships when one person tries to compel the other person to conform to a single way of being." Steve's adaptability—another trait of ADD adults—allows him to find creative ways to honor their differences.

Future Memories: Psychic Phenomenon or Vivid Motivator?

Steve's future memories—such as those showing him that his future happiness involved Helene—actually drive him to make his dreams a reality. Future memories may seem incredible. Indeed they are. This is the same phenomenon Paul Orfalea described when he told his teachers in third grade that he didn't need to learn to write because he would own a large business and his secretaries would do all the writing for him. It is the same phenomenon that led Hagen (profiled in chapter 8) to start his own business despite not having had any previous business experience. He didn't question whether or not he would be successful because he already had a clear vision of his success.

Is this phenomenon a psychic ability or something else? By Steve's account, it may just be the ability to create mental pictures that are so compelling that they seem indisputably real. The clarity of these images then creates a driving force that allows the person to plow through obstacles and doubts. At any rate, it seems likely that this ability is linked directly to ADD. Both a failure to pay attention to details and a strong drive to take action can be connected to the power of future memories. Indeed, it may be that the spaciness and dreaminess of ADD are due to a vivid inner world that is more than a match for the real world in intensity.

In terms of the motivating force of future memories, Steve told me that, because these vivid images seem so very real, once he has experienced a future memory he blots out everything else. In his opinion this may explain the impulsive, driven quality of ADD adults: once you've seen the future, you're less likely to pay attention to the here and now—something that could make a person seem from the outside both driven and distracted.

"It's like living with the fast-forward button pressed much of the time," said Steve. "As well as being spacey and disconnected from the present, I find that I start to do everything too fast—eating, walking, driving, everything. Apparently I used to walk down the street seemingly engaged in some deep, animated conversation with an invisible 'other person.' My lips and my facial expressions would shift rapidly as I fast-forwarded through a planned discussion with someone. I must have looked completely insane!"

Herein lies an interesting and never before suggested explanation for the ADD failure to pay attention: the entire present experience is completely neglected in the face of creating a future that matches future memories.

How Future Memories Lead to Great Parenting

Every mother and father knows the age-old rub of being a parent: you sacrifice your life for your child but get no thanks for your efforts, at least not while they are young. Steve's ability to clearly envision the future offers him an interesting solution to this age-old dilemma, providing him with the fuel for being a great parent. Steve has two daughters, aged fourteen and seventeen. Both have ADD traits and struggle with the performance demands of school. Although they are very talented, typical ADD issues often makes managing their behavior difficult.

Steve acknowledges that although he is devoted to his children, they do not always thank him for his efforts. He does not expect any gratitude. However, because he has this ability to see clear, filmlike clips of the future, he realized that in order to have the relationship with his children he wants in the future, he needs to be involved and devoted now, despite the natural challenges of child rearing. He can also envision the gratitude his children will feel in the future, though, like all kids, they now take their parents for granted. Steve can see twenty, thirty, and even forty years ahead—times when his daughters will appreciate what he gave them as children.

When he earns his children's ire because he has set limits for them, he sees clearly how the discipline he puts in place now will create the characters they will have in the future. Because he can envision how his children will be, he can also see what they need now to create their ideal future. So his parenting skills and his ability to guide and set limits are all directly related to his ability to vividly see these future memories.

Like any gift, future memories have a downside. Steve reports that because he uses the future to propel his parenting, it can sometimes be very difficult for him to stay in the present. During the early days of his separation from Jeanette, she would often pick up negative emotions from the kids because, she said, although he was spending time with them, "You're simply not really there—and they feel it." Because he recognizes his impulsiveness, he disciplines himself to stay present as much as possible, but admits that getting so wrapped up in the future can make this hard to do sometimes.

It may help you to recognize that, although you may have a hard time with some elements of parenting (like sitting still with your children), you also have the capacity to be a great parent. Future memories can provide you with important motivation for discipline and setting limits—or just for spending time with your kids.

Alternative Living Arrangements

Finding creative ways to adapt to ADD is a common characteristic of adults with ADD, and Steve is no exception. He and Helene maintain separate homes a half mile apart to preserve their relationship and love for each other. Helene describes Steve as "the most chaotic person I have ever met." Steve acknowledges that he is indeed messy and chaotic, and that his home is filled with clutter because he likes to hoard things. Helene, on the other hand, is neat and tidy. Having separate living quarters allows them to keep their love alive without being unduly stressed by Steve's disorganization. This arrangement also allows Steve and his children to have a space all their own.

This unique solution not only addresses the problem of their different styles, it also helps Steve thrive. Like many ADD adults, Steve does better under his own structure than under societal standards. He told me, "Society tries to repress a lot of things—people are repressed about all types of things. The concept of getting married but not living in the same house is abnormal to some people." He admitted he gets a kick out of stepping outside the bounds, "I don't want to be told anything. I want to start each day with a clean sheet of paper. What's comfortable for me is having an awful lot of unknowns." For Steve it's liberating to break normal structures; indeed, doing things the old-fashioned way takes a toll on him. He is quick to point out, however, that his alternative living arrangements aren't simply for the sake of defiance. Rather, they are in the service of a deeper urge to live in harmony despite different personal habits, even though that may be hard for other people to see. This arrangement allows him to break free from something that wouldn't serve him well, and allows both him and Helene to enjoy each other without creating unnecessary conflicts about personal habits.

Emotional Intensity

In his relationships, Steve demonstrates two of the major gifts of adult ADD: emotional intensity and interpersonal intuition. Helene described him in an e-mail as "generous, with flashes of absolute brilliance; he's loving, caring, considerate (to a point), driven, and unafraid (in terms of his own abilities). He sometimes picks up on the fact that there's something wrong before I even notice that I'm down in the dumps."

Helene also noted that Steve has both a deep compassion for others and a tendency to get emotionally involved very quickly. As an example, she described his involvement with an elderly neighbor. It wasn't the neighbor's family but Steve who contacted her doctor and helped arrange for her to be taken to a convalescent home.

Steve explained to me that this emotional sensitivity can lead to one of the signal traits of ADD: distractibility. For example, he described how, during corporate management meetings, his attention would veer away from whomever was speaking. Instead, for long periods of time his mind would meander about the room, pondering the lives and personal situations of the various individuals present. If a colleague came under attack during a meeting, he would often concentrate more on what was going on at a personal level for that colleague than on what was actually being said. He would constantly read others' feelings, wanting to protect them from getting hurt. But if, at that same meeting, Steve were suddenly asked for an opinion or contribution, he could usually deliver an insight that demonstrated that, even though he hadn't seemed to be listening or paying attention, he had completely absorbed what was going on. (Often to the frustration of his critical peers!)

While this emotional sensitivity is a great gift, Steve also directly links it to his inability to listen: "I find I can read others very well—I put myself in their shoes and take on their emotions. This may be a gift but it's also very damaging, as I find myself 'soaking up' emotions like sadness and pain from others." Steve is often so tuned in to what is unspoken that he doesn't take in any words. Unfortunately, this can disrupt his relationships. The deep irony is that he is actually highly attuned to the people he is with, just not in a way that other people recognize or find socially acceptable.

In a further elaboration of how this quality affects him and his relationships, he wrote in an e-mail to me, "Today I still suffer from this 'symbiosis' effect and have problems letting go—leaving others to get on by themselves and just being me. I just keep connecting to others' needs and feeling their emotions. It's so draining sometimes. Of course, the flip side is that I am able to read people and situations very well, which has helped me in business. And being 'sensitive' to others allows me to relate well to others. But the downside is that people latch onto me when they see/feel my empathy."

This gift was identified in Steve's management assessment results: he was pegged as the highest functioning executive on interpersonal communications. Indeed, at higher levels of business, interpersonal skills are some of the most valued management and leadership abilities. Steve's aptitude for understanding the needs of others allowed him to deliver results to his superiors and gain credibility and acceptance on his way up the corporate ladder. In addition, because he understood others' needs and concerns so well, he was able to strongly motivate team members.

It seems counterintuitive that emotional sensitivity and interpersonal intuition could constitute a "deficit disorder" in relationships. However, in many settings, we think of a person who is paying attention to us as listening to the words we're saying and being able to continue the conversation in a direction seen as "on topic." Steve's way of connecting to others, on the other hand, often gives him the appearance of not listening—a social deficit—when, in fact, he is deeply engaged, just in a different way. Indeed, his emotional sensitivity can cause him to tune in at a deep level, while missing the exact words spoken.

It's also easy to see how this emotional intensity can show up in school as a performance deficit. A child tuned in to the emotional lives of the teacher and nearby students might well find it almost impossible to focus on the single stream of incoming information that must be retained to perform well academically. On another level, the ADD student may also be demonstrating a sensitive relational gift when acting as the class clown. In doing so, the ADD student may be feeling the need of classmates for entertainment—and meeting that need to her own detriment. Indeed this is precisely how Steve described his time in school. He explained that he avoided school because "being with large groups of children just drained me. I found school emotionally tiring—so many relationships to manage. I was often told off by teachers, either for being a dreamer and easily distracted, or for being too chatty."

Steve's story, however, illustrates how this deficit can be translated into a gift. Let's step outside of Steve's story for a moment to set forth this translation clearly.

If you are an adult, you may avoid social settings because they are too draining for you. Your relational gifts can lead people to become too attached to you or make too many demands. Similarly, you may find it difficult to spend time with your kids because your sensitivity to their needs is so intense that you become overwhelmed.

Interpersonal intuition and emotional sensitivity can be either gifts or symptoms. In settings that rely on interpersonal connections rather than information gathering, interpersonal intuition and emotional sensitivity can be great gifts. In settings where people expect you to pay attention to details or gather information, they can become deficits. The take-home message is straightforward: any trait—even a symptom—may be either a gift or a deficit, depending on the demands of the situation and setting.

ADD Adults Can Break Limiting Beliefs for Their Kids

ADD adults also have a great gift to offer their children: freedom from the belief that how you do in school determines your success in life. Because Steve did so poorly in school, dropping out at the age of sixteen, but still went on to great success in business, he gained a perspective that many of today's parents do not have: a child's ability to be happy and successful isn't the same thing as her performance in school.

Because both of his daughters have ADD traits, they both find school life difficult. Steve's own success story shows his daughters that by focusing on what they are good at, they will find success and happiness in life. Thanks to his own experiences, Steve is able to teach them that it's possible to capitalize on ADD traits to create success in spite of failures at school.

Like many adults, Steve discovered his own ADD diagnosis through his child's. His younger daughter was diagnosed as having ADHD at age twelve, having struggled throughout her primary school years with behavioral issues and an inability to thrive.

Recognizing many of her symptoms in himself, he dug out his old school reports and found data consistent with ADD. From age five on, he received teacher comments on performance and behavioral difficulties that today would easily be recognized as constituting ADD:

> "Disappointing ... partly out of inefficiency but also partly out of laziness."
>
> "He needs to work harder than most."
>
> "Erratic."
>
> "Rather careless."

"He could have done even better if he did not play around in class."

"He appears to dream."

"He lets himself down by a lack of factual detail."

In an e-mail to me, Steve described his failure in school:

My big problem was trying to adapt to the rigid structure. There was no flexibility. You simply had to fit in. If you didn't you'd have a miserable time, it was as simple as that. For a child with a vivid imagination, endless creativity, and emotional intelligence it was stifling. In some ways I probably became aloof, [because I saw] the stupidity of a system out of date and out of touch with the needs for the future that I had seen for myself ... It was not just the school that was the problem, but the education system as a whole. The national curriculum of subjects deemed important to every child left me cold and disinterested. I didn't see what was so exciting, or useful, about trying to absorb thousands of facts over a five-year period and then repeat them all in the correct order during a two-hour exam in a big hall. I felt that I was being tasked with things I was not good at—yet

> *was offered no alternative. In those days your exam performance was everything.*

Steve's failure in school and cynical questioning of its relevance to his life are typical of the ADD child. What's interesting is that, although Steve's failures in school were ascribed to qualities in him, testing of these same qualities years later would peg him as an extremely gifted, able, and intelligent executive.

Steve's story offers a dramatic example of how what looks like failure in one setting may be the result of a gift that will lead to great success in another. If you are an adult struggling with memories of punishments and failures at school, it is time to tell a new story about who you are.

In reflecting on Steve's story, I can't help wondering how his great talents—talents that made him top gun among a group of highly successful executives—could have gone unrecognized for so long. While the answer to this question goes far beyond the scope of this book, it does point to a societal neglect of noticing, observing, and rewarding relationship skills. This focus on what is wrong, rather than what is right, is a global phenomenon, observed in every country polled by Gallup testing (Buckingham and Clifton 2001). Even the most medically minded health care providers point to the "charisma" and "charm" of adults and kids with ADD. If you put your own charm and charisma front and center of your life—and become a strong advocate for your other ADD gifts, too—you will sow the seeds for a powerful transformation.

PART II

The Five Gifts of Adult ADD

CHAPTER 5

Creativity: Cultivate Your Daydreams

There may be a direct connection between your sloppy mistakes and your creativity. Your sloppy mistakes may be due, in part, to a willingness to experiment, to try new things. So, too, may your creativity. Your sloppiness may also be related to your capacity to loosen your perception of the world. So, too, may your creativity. Being concerned with getting things precisely right may come from a different part of the brain than creativity, and may interfere with it. On the other hand, perceiving each moment as a possibility to be experienced rather than a concrete reality to be controlled will naturally lead to creativity—and sloppiness.

Cognitive science tells us that even the mechanics of perception are in part creative. This means that how we see the world—and even *what* we see—is always in part created by us. At the most basic level, optical illusions—for example, a drawing that can alternately be seen as a duck or a rabbit—show us how we create what we see. One day, while I was driving my kids up a mountain, my son asked me if I had ever seen a house get smaller. He was pondering how our perception changes as we get farther away and higher up. If as adults we don't perceive a house getting smaller, that is in part because we adjust our perception of reality from what we know. These are basic examples but still show that perception involves creativity.

Artistic creativity tends to be common in ADD adults. ADD adults are often artists, musicians, designers, stylists, and entertainers. Artistic creativity may be related to the very same sloppiness that gets ADD adults in trouble. Think of the great visual artists of the last two centuries, artists who have shown us images of a world we have never seen with our own eyes. How many of us have seen the swirling sky in van Gogh's *Starry Night,* the odd shapes in Picasso's art? We don't call their representations sloppy, we call them genius. Now if you could only get your employees or bosses to see the genius in *your* visions...

Even if you are not artistic in the formal sense, ADD adults bring this element of creativity to everything they do, in both their work and their relationships. Creativity has been termed a form of *divergent thinking,* meaning it opens up possibilities rather than nailing them down with rigid definitions (McCrae 1987). Are mistakes and sloppiness anything less than perceiving the world in a way that opens up possibilities? It's true that mistakes can lead to unfortunate consequences in the real world, but at a basic level mistakes and sloppiness are rooted in a way of looking at the world as in part unformed rather than as a done deal. Are Picasso's misshapen and deformed humans mistakes? Or does he see differently—and perhaps more deeply—than the rest of us?

Psychologists have long seen meaning in mistakes. Freud's psychopathology of everyday life shows us that a verbal mistake—what has become known as a Freudian slip—will often reveal what we really think. As one classic joke puts it, a Freudian slip is "saying one thing and meaning your mother." Once, after my husband offered me some constructive criticism, I began to retort, "That was just an insult!" but instead unintentionally blurted out, "That was just an insight!" My mistake revealed a deeper truth. Just as creativity can reveal deeper truths about who you are and how you see the world, so too can your sloppiness and mistakes.

Legend has it that David Neeleman, the founder of JetBlue and a fellow adult with ADD, invented electronic ticketing to solve his own problem with losing airline tickets. His mistakes became grist for inventiveness.

ADD adults are notorious for social missteps ranging from insensitive comments to embarrassing outbursts. The same failure to follow social norms can lead to the creation of a new culture or new standard within a culture. An emotional person in a corporate culture may set a new standard of expressiveness. A member of a spiritual counterculture who touts the benefits of being rich and ambitious may similarly change the community's expectations and perspective. Additionally, a person who is sloppy and loose in speech may just be saying what others are thinking but are too constrained to say themselves. This vocalization is good for all of us: the more information a system has available to it—the less that is hidden—the more effective it will be in adapting to existing realities and meeting its goals while fulfilling its own values.

LIFE IS MESSY

Your mistakes, messes, and sloppiness may also be part of your creativity. A lack of organization—not just a lack of organizing skills, but a lack of organizing ability—may be one of the fundamental deficits of ADD. As discussed in chapter 1, your brain may be structured differently, so that rather than being directed by a central executive function, you are driven by whims, impulses, and erratic feelings. For example, while driving a date to a movie, you might see a hot air balloon over your head and decide to follow it in your car. As you set off on an exciting adventure, your movie plans fall to the wayside. However, this sort of disruption doesn't bother you; in fact, you thrive on it. Your date may feel differently—enchanted if she's in love with you, irritated if she can't stand switching plans at the last minute. It is the impulse you have to follow your whims that also lays the foundation for a creative life—encompassing both a creative approach to solving problems and artistic creativity.

The medical model's insistence that mistakes, messes, and sloppiness are signs of dysfunction may be all wrong. Not only may these qualities be directly related to creativity, they may also have value in themselves. One study found that individuals whose desks were very neat were actually less productive than those with messier desks (Abrahamson and Freedman 2007). They spent more time organizing and less time producing. Messes can have other benefits as well: When a folder is properly filed, its information is out of sight and out of mind. But if you tolerate messes and keep piles of notes, papers, and files around, you may stumble across important information at the right time—or at least be more likely to keep it present in your mind than if it were in a filing cabinet.

Creativity involves the synthesis of disparate pieces of information in new ways. If you have piles around you, your mess may place different pieces of information next to each other—and provoke a brilliant idea for combining approaches or elements. Thus, having piles or being messy can not only keep information closer at hand for longer periods of time, it can also allows different arenas of your life to collide—both literally and figuratively.

ACTIVITY: FIND THE MESSAGE IN YOUR MESSES

Believe it: There is a method to your madness. In this activity you'll use your mess to generate a creative approach to a problem you're struggling with.

1. Write out a question you would like to find a creative answer to. (This will work best if your question is focused on only a single issue. Also, try to avoid using the word "should" in your question since that can limit your creativity. Rather than asking for a "right" answer, ask for guidance to the next step. "Should" implies a rigid standard for you to conform to; in creative problem solving there are, by definition, many possible "right" next steps.)

2. Find a mess or pile that is out of control. Pick up as much of the pile as is comfortable and begin flipping through its contents. Read through the pile at your own pace, giving time only to what draws your attention.

3. Think of your question. Have any new answers or new ways of looking at your problem come to

you? If you're still stuck, go through the pile again; look for anything that could relate to your problem.

4. Don't worry about coming up with a right answer; instead, reflect on what in your messy pile captured your interest; write out one or two possible next steps related to these items that grabbed you.

To come up with an example for you, I used this activity to find some wisdom in the messes I berate myself for. I reflected on a collaboration I was involved in that had become stuck for reasons that weren't clear to me. My question was "What next step should I take to facilitate this collaboration?" I have a system for making sure important papers don't get lost, but I also have a hodgepodge of completely unrelated papers sitting in a stack on the floor. The things that drew my attention as I leafed through this stack were a thank-you card I had received for a gift and some notes on a compromise my husband and I had made about dividing up household chores. Putting these two together, I came up with the idea to go out of my way to thank the other person in the stalled collaboration for what he was doing while formally outlining who was responsible for what and making sure that we weren't both doing the same thing. This was a promising new next step—and one I wouldn't have generated on my own.

THE IMPULSE TO CREATE

Creativity demands an element of daring and impulsiveness. A person who creates is realistic enough to know the boundaries of what is normative, impulsive enough to constantly be jumping on the other side of that line, and daring enough to push it in other people's faces.

The creative urge is an impulse itself. When ADD adults behave impulsively, in many cases they are simply expressing their creativity. Indeed, impulsiveness may be irretrievably mixed up with creativity. In defining it as part of a disorder, with little reflection on what it is and where it comes from, the medical model has gone too far.

Where *does* an impulse come from? From a clinical view, it is likely that it comes from the unconscious. Many psychologists and spiritual teachers have drawn a direct connection between creativity and the unconscious. Think of your unconscious as all your thoughts, feelings, and instincts that don't jibe with your current "tribal beliefs" and so get pushed away from your experience. In this understanding there is substantial overlap between the unconscious and the impulsive. In many cases, I have observed that an impulse is simply an urge to do something you are not supposed to do.

If an impulse is often merely an urge to do something you are not supposed to do, then the medical model of psychology is little more than a rigid taskmaster wagging its finger while tsk-tsking. Calling impulsiveness a psychological symptom is bit like saying, "I told you not to do what you're not supposed to do." Who knew psychology was such an old maid?

Indeed, impulsiveness may actually come from a need to counterbalance the rigidity of what is not allowed. A friend's boyfriend jumped off a cruise ship while it was docked. Why? He told her he had an uncontrollable urge. His unconscious seems to have been driven to disrupt the sense-dulling pampering he'd received on the cruise ship. His impulse to break the rules was a sign of his life force desperately seeking an identity independent of the shiny, happy lifestyle of the cruise.

While jumping off a cruise ship doesn't add value to the world, impulses often do. Michelangelo's impulse to cut open corpses to see what was inside led to breathtaking masterpieces of art that startle us with their humanity. Rosa Park's impulse to dig her heels in and refuse the ridiculous insistence that she move led to advances in civil rights that changed the world. Art, science, technology, and development are all moved forward by impulse.

We all know impulsiveness has a dark side. But how much of this dark side is actually caused by tension between the expression and repression of impulses? Impulsiveness gets a bad name because it often goes hand in hand with addictive behaviors. Much of the destruction linked to impulses—the violence and recklessness—occurs under the influence of drugs and alcohol. But what if these addictive behaviors are actually futile attempts to dull into submission impulses seeking healthy and daring expression? If so, the culprit behind the destruction isn't the impulse but the failure of the courage needed to give birth to it.

While impulsiveness can lead to one set of problems, fear of making a mistake can lead to another. Fear of making a mistake can paralyze a person, causing the person to live a sterile life. Impulsiveness includes a certain willingness to make mistakes—which in some situations can be essential, even lifesaving. People who are afraid to make mistakes tend to focus on what may go wrong, what already has gone wrong, and what they cannot do. Adults with ADD are more likely to jump at the ideas that flash through their mind without fully examining possible risks. Both of these ways of being in the world are valuable; their particular usefulness depends on the setting or situation.

IMAGINATION: ENCHANTED BY WHAT MAY BE

The single most important factor in creativity is imagination. In order to bring something new into the world, you have to be able to first imagine it. Imagination is the ability to dwell on what is not real or not yet real. It is the ability to the let the mind wander away from what is known to generate things not yet known. Many of the symptoms of ADD can be seen as the side effects of deep imagination.

Picture This

The key deficit of ADD is distractibility. But what distracts the ADD person? In addition to emotional sensitivity, in some cases it's the person's imagination. Perhaps you've lost interest in what is because you are enchanted by what may be. To imagine is to put your attention on a fleeting fantasy with no material substance. To focus is to keep your attention on something. Focus leads to follow-through. Distraction leads to exploration and creation. Boredom is a powerful impetus for bringing something new into the world.

This brings us to another ADD symptom: impatience. Impatience is a hallmark of the ADD adult. You may be crippled by boredom, irritated by delays, totally incapable of delaying gratification. This impatience can be a trigger for imagination. If the world isn't stimulating enough for you, impatience can lead you to create for yourself your desired gratification, if only in your mind. (If all good things come to those who wait, perhaps all good ideas come to those who can't stand to wait!)

Guess What You Just Did

Many people think of fantasies as predominantly about sex. Fantasizing is actually the process of generating possible scenarios, usually related to the fulfillment of a desire. In reality, you have fantasies all the time about things that have nothing to do with sex. Any daydream about wanting to be in another place and time, or of goals coming true, is a fantasy. You might have a fantasy about a vacation, a better future, or space creatures from different planets hanging out in an intergalactic bar. If you're a person who has a rich inner world—someone who can generate a lot of fantasies—you'll find it hard to pay attention to the real world. Who can listen to an employee droning on defensively when intergalactic bars and tropical vacations are just waiting to be imagined?

Psychologists use the word "fantasy" all the time, often in nonsexual ways. Fantasies can reveal directions for healing and personal development by showing you needs and wants that you may not fully admit to yourself. For example, I will often ask a teenager trying to make major life choices, "What fantasies do you have about this choice?" Fantasies about choices can provide essential information for making decisions. Fantasies may show that what moments before seemed the easiest, most promising route is actually a trap. Or they may reveal something as unexpectedly positive. When a client wondered if he was moving too quickly in a relationship, I guided him through a vivid fantasy of moving forward toward greater commitment; his emotional reaction was one of great exhilaration. He thus answered his own question.

This example reveals a deeper point—fantasies have a truth of their own. We think of fantasies as by definition false. But fantasies aren't concerned with true or false, they're concerned with creation. Fantasies guide you in creating reality, not in reflecting it. ADD gives you lots of fantasies. These can distract you, but they can also give you the power to create a new world rather than repeat your past. The symptom is tied up with the gift.

ACTIVITY: FANTASY ISLAND

This activity will give you the experience of accessing fantasies to reveal new directions for your life. Don't worry about whether or not you're doing this right, or whether the fantasy or image that comes to you is right or wrong.

1. Set aside fifteen minutes when you won't be disturbed. If you have any concerns or worries, write them down on a piece of paper and tell yourself that you will return to them in fifteen minutes, when the activity is over.

2. If you're at home, lie down as if to take a nap. If you're somewhere else, stare out the window or just let your mind wander. Don't try to make anything happen. If a worry comes into your mind, tell yourself that you'll get back to it when the activity is over.

3. Let your mind wander, and say to yourself, "What I really need now is..." If your mind starts to return to real-world problems and logistics, gently guide yourself back to your fantasy. Repeat this sentence stem if you need to: "What I really need now is..." Because you're not concerned with right or wrong, let as many answers come into your mind as possible. Don't stop at just one or two answers. After you have several answers, let your mind wander into a fantasy or daydream.

4. You can encourage a vivid fantasy by letting yourself elaborate on whatever appears in your

mind. If you've discovered that you need a vacation, generate specific images of that vacation—whether it will be adventuresome or relaxing, in warm or cold weather, alone or with a group. Once you get a scene or image or movielike fantasy, just go with it. Let it play out as long as you have time.

5. Write down the fantasy that came to you. If you only got words or thoughts, don't be disappointed; write these down. If you got a glimpse of an image or a feeling, write these down, too—these can be hugely important.

6. If you get an answer that you don't like, write it down. I once had a client produce a very clear fantasy about what he needed, but he said he couldn't follow the exercise because his fantasy was blocked by a clear, precise image. He said he couldn't get beyond this picture in his mind. It was obvious to me that the image that was blocking his answer *was* the answer. The image that came to his mind was of a person whom he desperately needed but was rejecting because of his fear of dependency.

7. Once you have your fantasy or daydream, find a way to bring it into reality. No matter what it is, find a way to immediately honor it and begin to make it real. When working to bring your fantasy to life, both quick, small gestures and long-term

plans are important. For example, when I found myself having repetitive fantasies of an old-fashioned summer—bike rides, beaches, lying in the grass, being idle without a care—I first made myself a glass of lemonade (a strong symbol of summertime for me) and then started to plan some lazy summer activities and recreational fun.

ARTIST DEFICIT DISORDER

Is it possible that the high rates of ADD diagnosis will soon reflect a culture-wide "artist deficit disorder"? With the SAT as the coin of the realm in parenting circles, many parents actively dismiss kids' interests in artistic vocations. As standards for achievement have become more rigid and performance demands have increased, the value placed on the cultivation of visual, musical, and dramatic arts has decreased.

However, as I regularly tell my ADD clients, the world needs artists. For many people the urge, talent, and inclination to create art is obvious and compelling. Still, they often push away artistic urges for one reason: "I won't make any money as an artist." (We'll explore this limiting belief below—it can be turned around.) There are actually many resources for learning how to be a successful artist. Even if you don't make art your profession, honoring your artistic urges can transform the rest of your life. When you give expression to your artistic side, you free up energy that can feed the rest of your life. Because repressing or denying your creativity sucks up your life force, just unleashing this energy can change your life.

Who Wants to Be an Artist and a Millionaire?

Marc Allen is a multimillionaire, the president of a publishing company, an author, and a musician. His whole life, Marc knew he could only do what he loved. Until he was thirty years old, he played in rock bands and worked with theater groups, living in poverty but having the time of his life. On his thirtieth birthday, he decided he wanted to do what he loved, in his own style, but also be a millionaire. He wanted to be able to sleep late and not work Mondays. He tells the journey he made from poverty to wealth in his book *The Type-Z Guide to Success: A Lazy Person's Manifesto for Wealth and Fulfillment* (New World Library, 2006).

Before the age of thirty, Marc followed his artistic impulses and went from theater group to rock band. He was fired from every job he had. He learned from his frequent job changes what made bad bosses bad. He promised himself that when he was a boss he wouldn't be a petty tyrant, wouldn't treat employees like children; instead, he would seek to improve productivity by being reasonable. Today he is the president of New World Library. In a personal interview I had with him in July of 2007, he advised those who struggle to keep a job, "If you are going from job to job, it may be that there are important lessons you are learning; try to figure out if there is a pattern or skill set or repeated lesson you are learning." In Marc's case the simple fact of being fired many times gave him great preparation for his job as president of a company. By moving from job to job he was able to observe many different styles of leadership and determine for himself what was effective and what was not.

Although Marc hasn't been diagnosed with ADD and doesn't display any impairment in functioning, he has faced many of the same challenges as ADD adults. He is quite open about his disorganization and insists that if you do the inner work he recommends (examples follow)—what he calls the "core belief process"—you can overcome a history of failure and terrible organization skills. In my interview with him, he told me that when people ask him how he became so successful and if they can be, too, he tells them, "Look at how disorganized I am. I don't have it together and yet I make millions and publish successful books." He rules by his gut, not his head. He shared a powerful example of this with me: "When I read the first few lines of *The Power of Now,* I got a tingling sensation. I knew I would publish this book and it would be big. I know within seconds or minutes if I will publish something or work with someone." Working from quick instincts rather than a laborious attention to details—a trait shared by many ADD adults—has been the cornerstone of Marc's success.

Like Paul Orfalea and Steve Prevett, Marc also experienced a distinct future memory. One day, while he was still a theater student in high school, he was walking through the hall when a future memory came to him very clearly: "I have something to say. I'm going to be a writer." It didn't make any sense at the time, but it was very clear and he knew it would be true. It would be another fifteen to twenty years before he began to write.

His inspirational story challenges the belief that you have to work hard and follow someone else's rules to enjoy financial success. Through his core belief process, Marc turned his whole life around in just a few years. As Marc tells the story, the breakthrough came with certain key words he learned from Catherine Ponder's book *The Dynamic Laws of Prosperity* (1962): "in an easy and relaxed manner, in a healthy and positive way." Many people believe that achieving success has to be hard and challenging. Marc realized that by saying these words before and after every affirmation, he could challenge this belief and instead start to believe that he could achieve success his way. The problem for Marc, as with many artists, was that he wanted success, but successful creativity requires a certain amount of wandering to discover and incubate your inspirations. A hard-driving lifestyle does not fit well with artistic creativity.

Even though Marc was living the life of his dreams in rock bands and theater groups, he had acquired some nasty beliefs that were holding him back from financial success. His breakthrough solution was to write down these limiting beliefs and translate them instead into empowering beliefs. For example, he transformed his limiting belief "I am a fool with money. I am out of control. I am heading for trouble" by affirming regularly, "I am sensible and in control of my finances. I am creating total financial success in an easy and relaxed manner, in a healthy and positive way."

If you're an artist and you want to be a millionaire, you may need to first overcome limiting beliefs about your lifestyle, how success is achieved, and the myth of the starving artist. The following are some core belief transformations for you to experiment with. You might consider adding the phrase suggested by Marc Allen, "in an easy and relaxed manner, in a healthy and positive way," at the end of each new belief, a phrase he attributes to Catherine Ponder.

Limiting belief: It's noble to be a starving artist.

New belief: I am loving using the wealth I've earned as an artist to support, at the highest level, the production and distribution of my vision throughout the world in an easy and relaxed manner, in a healthy and positive way.

New belief: I am loving using my wealth to gain access to the best resources, teachers, and mentors to take my creative expression to the next level in an easy and relaxed manner, in a healthy and positive way.

New belief: I am loving using the wealth I've earned through my art to support other starving artists financially in an easy and relaxed manner, in a healthy and positive way.

New Belief: I am loving being so financially successfully that I serve as a role model for artists, proving that you can be a highly successful artist and a millionaire in an easy and relaxed manner, in a healthy and positive way.

New Belief: I am loving being able to use the wealth I've earned as an artist to travel to exotic locales and take luxurious retreats to nurture my inspiration in an easy and relaxed manner, in a healthy and positive way.

CREATIVITY OUTSIDE OF THE ARTS

Every professional calling requires creativity to some measure. Even if you have no interest in a paintbrush and no flair for design, you can still bring your ADD gift of creativity to bear in what you do. The success story below shows how creativity can be put to use in saving lives and putting out fires.

Captain Scott Ohlrich: The Creativity of Saving a Life

While most people may not think of firefighters as creative, Captain Scott Ohlrich would argue differently. Scott has read widely about ADD, trying to understand himself and gain tools for leading his crew, many of whom he believes also display the symptoms and gifts of ADD. In chapter 2 we met Scott and used firefighters to illustrate the idea that if you find a perfect match for your ADD symptoms, you may never suffer any impairment in functioning. Neither Scott nor his firefighters have been diagnosed with ADD; however, they fit the profile and symptom checklist. After my book *The Gift of ADHD* was released in 2005, Scott and I began to exchange e-mails; we spoke on the phone specifically for this profile in August of 2007.

Scott described himself as "one of those kids who spent a lot of time staring out the window during class." He doesn't chalk this up as wasted time, though. He remembers watching the trajectories of leaves falling from the tall oak trees in the schoolyard, comparing them to the flights of paper airplanes he'd throw out the window when the teacher left the room. At his parochial school, both staring out the window and throwing paper airplanes elicited corporal punishment. But for Scott, "exploring this relationship was worth the pain and humiliation, as it was far more interesting than discussing the proper use of adjectives."

Scott's interests reflected his life calling. As it turned out, he wouldn't need to know the proper use of adjectives.

Reading the Smoke

Why would the trajectories of leaves and the flights of paper airplanes be so interesting to Scott? What might these have to do with his destiny?

Firefighters are trained to read smoke as an indicator of events happening in the fire itself. "Everything about smoke—the color, the density, the 'push' or force, the direction of motion—tells us something," Scott explained. Firefighters use their observations about the pattern and "flight" of smoke to predict what the fire will do. "The idea being, if you can accurately anticipate what will happen next, you can intervene and change the outcome," said Scott. For Scott, reading smoke would turn out to be far more relevant to his life than reading books. Indeed, Scott's fascination with leaves and paper airplanes was actually training for his future life vocation. His early interest in air currents and their effects on objects directly relates to his ability to read smoke and make predictions about how a fire will be impacted by air currents. But by his report, he was punished for his "distraction."

"As I think back on it, I did have a few teachers in my school career who seemed to understand. I had a teacher in seventh grade who, instead of making me write the standard 'I will complete all my homework on time' one hundred times, would ask me to come up with 'one hundred uses for a butterfly wing'! I didn't know it at the time, but it was a far more thought-provoking and inspirational project. And when I completed it, I felt that I had actually accomplished something."

Interestingly, coming up with a one hundred uses for a butterfly wing is an example of brainstorming—one of the key techniques for generating creativity. Whereas linear thinking tries to identify a single correct answer, creative thinking generates many possible answers, judging these only after many options have been identified. This very same capacity—called divergent thinking—is fundamental to the job of the fire captain.

When a fire captain arrives at the scene of a fire, he cannot watch in horror as people on the street do; he must act. To act wisely, he must quickly weigh all the possible actions he can think of and determine which is the right one. As Scott explained it, this skill draws on creativity and the ADD ability to quickly scan a situation. "If we view creativity as seeing the possibilities and acting to change outcomes," said Scott, "then that is exactly what my peers and I do every day." He broke down this scanning ability for me, describing it as "the ability to pay attention to everything all the time. It is *not* focusing on the details; it is focusing on everything, *including* the details. And this is a skill that not everyone possesses."

This scanning ability may have been evolutionarily selected for—hunters in early human culture had to scan their whole environment, not just focus in on details. This same ability can be a matter of life and death for firefighters. As soon as the best possible course of action is determined, the fire captain and his crew spring into action.

Rules Are Obstacles

What does it take to save lives and put out fires? "Nearly every normal obstacle (rule) of society will be suspended and replaced by trust." This one sentence Scott wrote to me defines both firefighting and the way the mind of an ADD adult works.

Scott defines a "normal obstacle" as a rule. A firefighter doesn't knock on doors; he tears them down. Firefighters run through red lights and stop signs to get to the scene of an emergency. They tell people they cannot return to their own home after a fire. For the firefighter, society's rules are obstacles that need to be suspended. This insistence that rules are obstacles is typical of ADD adults.

Scott imagines that most firefighters think like ADD adults—quickly and outside the box. Despite not having all of the details and information they need, firefighters work in a highly coordinated and synchronized fashion. They have to work together to determine priorities, collect further information, and create a team plan. As Scott tells it, "Most of the time we make the decision to act well before we are 100 percent certain that we are doing the right thing. This is where the ADD skill set comes into play. Having the ability to take in many details in a rapid fashion allows us to predict potential outcomes with confidence that we will be 'close enough' to the right answer. We also know that we can easily change our plans if a particular course of action doesn't give us a positive result. Consequently, we are comfortable taking action when most people might prefer to wait for more information." To save a life or put out a fire you can't wait for directions.

Creativity, Scott explained, is the driving force behind the break-the-rules mentality of firefighters. He shared with me the story of a tragedy that could have been averted by creative problem solving:

> *I think most people get so hung up on what they think they can't do that they don't realize what they can do. I'm reminded of a call that I was on when I had less than six months on the job. It was an apartment fire in which a mother and two children lost their lives. After the fire, the investigator was interviewing the gentleman who lived in the apartment next door. He stated that he could hear the little girl crying for help on the other side of the wall in his bedroom. He tried, but couldn't enter the apartment because of the heavy smoke and heat. What he didn't think of was that he could have punched a hole in the drywall from his bedroom into the girl's room and pulled her to safety.*

It's easy to see why the man never thought of punching a hole in the drywall—it's a solution that requires creative, outside-the-box thinking. Additionally, because he didn't know anything about fires, even if he had thought of this solution he might have imagined it would endanger his own life. In Scott's analysis, by focusing on what he couldn't do, this neighbor paralyzed his capacity to consider other options. These other options would have been outside the box and inevitably required risk and daring. So much of life is like this. Even though life often requires us to take risks, our nature urges us to seek safe and easy solutions. We want the easy answer, and when it doesn't work we throw our hands in the air and say, "I tried." Scott's analysis reminds us that it's important—sometimes even vital—to focus on what you *can* do, rather than what you cannot.

Professions like firefighting, which require the suspension of conventional rules, demonstrate that the impulse to call rules "obstacles" can have great survival value. If breaking rules is important—as it is in firefighting, the arts, and innovation—what happens to people hardwired by biology and genetics not just to think outside the box, but to actively jump outside the box? Evidence suggests that education and moral values are increasingly pressuring us toward conformity, control, and performance demands (Levine 2006). I know from my clinical practice that those who are driven by unnamed forces—or forces named ADD—to push limits often arrive on the doorstep of adulthood bruised and battered by unrelenting criticism and punitive controls.

Risk a Lot to Save a Life

"Risk nothing to save nothing; risk a little to save a little; risk a lot to save a life" is a saying firefighters live by. In order to save a life, firefighters may need to work well outside of their training and very near the limits of their personal safety. ADD is characterized by impulsiveness, stimulation seeking, and risk taking. It seems almost a formula for creating a firefighter. Who else could tolerate the constant risk, the unknowns of each call, the high levels of stimulation entailed in facing a fire?

Scott believes that stimulation seeking may be related to creativity. He argues that the ability to quickly generate multiple scenarios is directly related to the adrenaline rush that ADD adults and firefighters may be hardwired to seek out. He sees a connection between this same rush and the medications used to treat ADD, stimulants much like the neurotransmitter adrenaline. Scott shared with me an e-mail from one of his firefighters, Aaron Adams: "I am aware of a difference in my perception of time as it seems to slow down, and I will literally run through and rule in or out a dozen possible mitigating actions in seconds." He attributes this shift in temporal perception to the adrenaline rush.

Aaron described a scene where an individual had stabbed himself and was still actively fighting another person. Once he arrived on the scene, Aaron contacted the police, gathered information, restrained the violent individual, and administered lifesaving medical care. By Aaron's account the entire sequence of events took under seven minutes but felt like twenty.

Aaron agrees with Scott that firefighting demands creativity, particularly in problem solving. Aaron described his job as "a never-ending supply of technical things we need to know paired with a never-ending supply of situations to try and apply them to. On top of that there is rarely a scheduled time [for us to] be called upon, and the venue could be anywhere from our community to New Orleans." It's easy to see how the never-ending need for stimulation and the demand to generate multiple lifesaving courses of action within minutes or seconds might be a good match for an ADD adult.

Scott elaborated on his theory of stimulation seeking and its relation to creativity: "I am of the belief that the time-slowing effect Aaron described is a function of a blast of adrenaline. I think it heightens our senses to the inputs of our surroundings. Then, in retrospect, time seems to have slowed down because we have taken in so much information that the time frame 'must have been' longer."

What If Firefighters Took Adderall?

If Scott is on to something—and neurochemically he is correct in linking adrenaline with pharmaceutical stimulants—this leads to some interesting speculation. One line of research has shown that if you give animals a neurotransmitter, they will be less motivated to engage in actions that naturally stimulate this chemical. For example, one study found that giving monkeys oxytocin (a neurochemical that generates intense positive feelings in nursing mothers) caused the monkeys to stop nursing their infants (Turner et al. 2002). If adults with ADD need intense situations to get their fix, how would their lives change if they were medicated? Would firefighters taking chemical stimulants be less inclined to jump into the middle of a fire or other dangerous scene?

By Scott's account, the natural adrenaline rush allows him and his firefighters to stay calm, to create the sensation of time slowing down as they take in huge chunks of information and generate many possible courses of action. Consider how very many important jobs require both creative problem-solving skills and a willingness to head straight into an emergency rather than run away from it. Maybe the ADD brain has an important function to serve in society just as it naturally is.

Scott has shown us that creativity plays a key role in what firefighters do. The more possibilities a fire-fighter can generate for approaching a fire, the more likely it is that the firefighter will be able to overcome any obstacles encountered. And the better a firefight-er can scan a scene, taking in details but not becoming fixated on them, the more effective the fire-fighter will be.

Who would have guessed that Scott's preoccupation with leaves falling and airplanes flying was building an interest in aerodynamics? It was also generating skills in close observation. In particular, his interest in leaves shows a connection and respect for the forces of nature, a gift of ADD we'll explore further in the next chapter. On a deeper level, a leaf falling from a tree is a potent image of the death and loss inevitable to the life cycle. Maybe as young Scott stared out the window at falling leaves, he was etching deep into his psyche a view of life and death that would give him the courage to face his future vocation's possibility of death. A possibility few of us could bear.

ACTIVITY: TRANSLATE DISTRACTIONS INTO DESTINY

Scott's childhood "distractions" trained him to observe closely interactions between objects and air currents—a skill that would later enable him to read smoke, saving lives and putting out fires. Although he was punished for these distractions, in hindsight they were clearly vital to his preparation for his life vocation. In this activity you will practice translating your own distractions into hobbies, interests, or even another vocation.

1. In your journal, make a list of five interests or activities that distract your from what you are "supposed to be doing." No matter how frivolous or unimportant an activity may seem, put it on the list. Whether it's watching sports on TV, reading trashy novels, or taking walks in the woods, take the activity seriously—put it on the list.

2. Give each of these five distractions an entire page in your journal. Write the distraction at the top of the page, and then list five jobs, activities, or hobbies that could build on it. For example, if you love sports, you could join a sports team or consider a career in sports broadcasting, journalism, or coaching, among many other possibilities. Write for as long as you want, freely associating on what your interest in sports could lead you to. (*Free association* means just letting your mind wander—it's like brainstorming; in this case, write down every mental connection to sports that you generate.)

3. Write a list of specific skills you are gaining by pursuing your distraction. Try to generate as many answers as possible. For example, by

watching sports you might gain skills in calculating probabilities, understanding the value of team play, and determining the effectiveness of strategies. Even just learning the rules of a game you'd like to play is a useful skill. Don't be too concerned with right or wrong—allow your mind to explore the possibilities.

4. Seriously consider that your distraction may have an important role to play in your destiny. Even if it leads to nothing more than a hobby or interest, this can serve to generate energy that fuels other areas of your life. And hobbies and interests can turn your life around in unexpected ways by introducing you to people who share your interests; among these might be someone who will become a significant other or a business partner. Make a commitment to translate your distraction into a concrete action step. Take this step within one week.

CHAPTER 6

The Trailblazer: The Gift of Ecological Consciousness

You're sitting in front of your computer, nervous and jumpy. You keep checking your e-mail, even though you're not sure what you're checking it for. You can't sit still. Your office is climate controlled but you want to be outside, even if it is too hot, too cold, or raining. Maybe you dismiss your urge to be outside as frivolous—being in nature, taking in the elements, seems like a luxury. And after all, you're a grown-up now, who needs recess?

You do.

The images that flash across your mind—of getting away from it all, of communing with nature—actually provide valuable guidance: you really do need more face time with the natural world. This urge to be in nature isn't just another symptom of your ADD, isn't just another distraction flitting across your mind like a gnat that won't go away. This urge may actually be hardwired into you to help you heal. Nature is very healing for most people. Too much computer-screen time can disrupt anyone's biorhythms, making sleep and restful relaxation difficult. Nature may be one way to restore this imbalance. If a connection to nature is an inherent need of ADD, you would be well served to take seriously the notion that "nature is medicine."

Research has shown that for children, playtime in nature can improve various ADD symptoms, including the ability to focus and the ability to follow directions (Taylor, Kuo, and Sullivan 2001). Even though these symptoms can also be gifts, the ability to balance ADD gifts with the skills to get by in other settings will give the ADD individual the power of choice. While similar research on adults hasn't yet been done, as an ADD adult you probably have a heightened need to be in nature. Nature affords you the opportunity of expansiveness without the energy drain of computers and other people. It can be hard to get the chance to let your soul unfurl into the wide-open spaces that it craves. Nature gives you that chance. Indeed, nature allows your spaciness to take on new dimensions.

As an ADD adult you are, as psychologist James Hillman has put it, a "wide-open sensitive soul" (1996, 126). In nature your sensitivity is absorbed without your being irritated. Nature allows the space for your imagination to run wild and free. Unlike settings that scream for your attention, the empty spaces of nature give your attention an arena to roam. Nature also gives you the opportunity to walk, run, climb, and hike—to fully expend your hyper physical energy. Some ADD adults describe themselves as so hyper they want to climb walls. Maybe they are quite literally meant to climb, jump, or otherwise stretch themselves. The natural world is an ideal place to do this.

NATURE IS MEDICINE

It's time for you to take your need to be in nature seriously. If you've gone the route of medication, take your need to be in nature equally seriously. Nature is medicine for ADD kids, and adults too.

In nature you will find the peaceful resonance you have been looking for. The organic world of trees, sky, and animals is free from the fakeness you see in the human world. In nature you can let your guard down. In nature what you see is what you get. The natural world—a world you can take in with all of your senses—never misleads or traps your mind in detours as the artificial world of technology does. Being in nature, you can connect instantly and deeply with what you see, sometimes feeling one with the organic world. Nature fulfills the need for a deep level of engagement that often goes unmet in the office or home. In nature you can slide easily into the world around you—and in nature you get no argument about it.

SHAKE THE SILLIES OUT

Nature is the ideal playground for your high energy levels. To journey anywhere in nature, you need to physically move. Navigating nature requires a certain amount of strength and vigor. You may have become dismissive of your hyperactivity, seeing it only as a regrettable flaw. It isn't a flaw; you have a genuine need to stay highly active. A natural landscape is thus the ideal setting for challenging yourself.

You may feel like you need to be moving to think. Many adults with ADD do. For some people, thinking and inspiration seem to be visceral activities—activities that are rooted in the body. When you move your body, you may be able to think more clearly or with more focus. Or your mind may wander as your body does, allowing you to mentally cover a lot of ground, thus enhancing your creativity. Many people who have gone on to be athletes were once thought to be hyperactive.

Imagine that your abilities to think and plan and understand the world all have a bodily component. As you move, so you think. Now picture a small child in a playpen. Such a child's mind and body can wander and wonder only so far before being frustrated by environmental boundaries. Now imagine that same small child, wandering through a forest with trees, flowers, rocks, and animals to engage and provoke thought.

In observing my own preschool-aged children, it has seemed to me that thought is not yet abstracted from movement—that thought is movement. I sense that as they roam wide-open spaces, they forge a certain inner depth that will later become the architecture of their abstract thinking. Even as adults we have the capacity to expand our mental capacity through physical extension. Nature provides the most space for such expansion. Indeed, it may be that for those with the biggest ideas and impulses, it is only in nature that resonance and even rest can be found.

Even as an adult, whether you work in a cubicle or the corner office with a view of the Pacific, are you not in a playpen? Does the computer screen allow you to connect with it, to engage with it? Does the computer screen help your mind to follow its line of thought? Although computers give you access to the wide world of the Internet and a seemingly endless tool kit for getting your work done—which may fuel your gift for multitasking—if you are a person who thinks while moving, you may need to remind yourself to refresh and reboot with a jaunt in nature.

Computers and other tools come with implicit demands: do, solve, figure it out. Nature comes with no demands, only a gentle admonishment: be. For most of us, even our loved ones don't give us the same freedom from expectations, the same permission to just be, that nature does.

ACTIVITY: WATCHING THE WORLD GO ROUND AND ROUND

No matter where you live, you can always look up and see the sky. The sky offers us immediate connection with the majesty of the natural world—and yet, few of us ever look up in wonder. As an ADD adult, the expansiveness of the sky can resonate with your free-spirited openness and spaciness. Just connecting with the sky can be very healing and offer you time for reflection. When you don't have the time to rest and watch the sky, simply remind yourself to look up frequently throughout the day for a small dose of nature.

1. Find a place on the ground that will give you a decent view of the sky and allow you to spread out without being disturbed. Just plop yourself down and watch the sky. (Use a blanket, pillow, or anything else that will increase your comfort.)

2. Allow your mind to roam as far and wide as it wants to. Imagine this as similar to letting a dog off the leash or giving a horse free rein. Let your energy level guide how long you do this for; when you get bored, give yourself permission to move on.

3. Recapture this experience throughout your day by glancing up at the sky. Even this brief connection will be calming and can trigger the roaming feeling you enjoyed during your lengthier experiment.

When you've done this experiment one or more times, observe the impact it has on you. Does it calm you down? Does it clear your mind or make you more able to listen to others? Pay attention to what changes for you when you give yourself this gift. The more you observe its healing power, the more you will allow yourself to indulge in what otherwise might seem a waste of time.

ADD ADULT, SEEKING SOLACE AND STIMULATION

Like many ADD adults, you have probably received more than your fair share of criticism. This deficit disorder didn't arrive on your doorstep wrapped in a pretty bow. The harshness of the words "deficit disorder" reflects the painful interactions you've experienced. From the people you care about you may frequently hear "You never listen," "Stop interrupting me," "off-color," and "inappropriate." In work settings you may hear "doesn't follow through," "easily distracted," or "makes sloppy mistakes."

Nature embraces you without offering any judgments at all. Nature accepts you as you are. While the rest of the world says "do," nature says "be." While the rest of the world tells you there's something wrong with you, nature tells you that differences aren't disorders. The delicate flower that gives off fragrance and the rock face with its immovable grandeur are different, but both are gifts.

Nature reflects your gifts back to you; for example, the torrent of ideas flooding your mind can be seen in waterfalls, rapid rivers, or strong winds. And in addition to offering connection without judgment, nature meets your need for stimulation. Nature offers you demanding hikes, stimulating windy and rainy conditions for a walk or jog, and rock faces that dare you to climb them.

ACTIVITY: TAKE A WALK ON THE WILD SIDE

Your need for wildness may get you in trouble in your relationships and work. Feed your need for nature by planning outdoor adventures close to home. You can get a sense of nature's wildness just by going outside when it's dark and stormy.

1. Give yourself some "roam time." Like any wild animal, you need to get out into nature and explore the terrain. Find a place that gives you lots of space to roam, whether that be an open soccer field, an outdoor track, a hiking trail, or a mountain range.

2. Try to get your roam time during bad weather. This will help you feel that you're testing your spirit and bonding with nature. Rain, sun, stars, heat, cold, snow—all are elements of nature. The intensity of inclement nature can match your own intensity and meet your basic need for stimulation. If you can do so safely, venture out into the dark to look at the stars.

3. Give yourself permission to let your inner state match your outer surroundings. If it's dark and stormy outside and you're alone in a place where you can jump, scream, or howl, do so. If you're plodding through three feet of snow with great difficulty, let your frustration and anger at all that is slowing you down in your life come out. Release that outburst you've been holding in for a long time. If you set out in extreme heat or dryness,

let your own despair or emptiness emerge to match your environment.

The preceding activity can help you fulfill your need to be in nature, your craving for stimulation, and your yearning to break the rules. If you have a habit you are trying to break, whether it's eating too much, excessive alcohol consumption, drug use, or some other addiction, use this activity as a substitute. When temptation strikes, plan a "walk on the wild side" or just scoot out the door and get moving. Many people with ADD develop drug and alcohol problems or other addictions to slow themselves down in an attempt to match the tempo and pace of other people. This activity fulfills many of the root causes of the addiction and will distract you from your cravings.

If you want to use this activity as a substitute for an addiction, try to make it second nature. When you get a craving, try to connect with the deeper need to let your mind wander and your body move. For example, many people smoke pot because it "frees their mind" and slows them down. Movement and time in nature will give you these same benefits. Many people also develop bad habits both to dull the pain of beating themselves up for not focusing and not being organized, and to feed the constant drive for stimulation. When you take your needs seriously, you will heal the self-hatred and begin to resolve the root causes of your addiction or bad habit

Wandering Mind and Moving Body

As a basic rule, letting your mind wander as your body moves is a simple, effective way to meet your main needs as an ADD adult. Small doses of a wandering mind and moving body will serve as medicine. Nature and activity have the benefits of giving you the ability to manage your ADD symptoms/traits/gifts without the potential for addiction or troublesome side effects. Indeed, noted ADD experts suggest that regular walks can be as effective as medication (Hallowell and Ratey 2005). By going on a walk or a wild adventure that meets almost all of your ADD needs—for nature, stimulation, breaking rules, unfettered attention, and physical movement—you give yourself a potent brew of healing medicine. Additionally, you'll stop beating yourself up for not sitting still or staying focused. This practice will allow you to honor the need to nourish and nurture your inner wild child—let her out to play!

As you translate your "symptoms" into real needs to be met, you will experience dramatic transformations. Notice how you feel before and after your wild ventures. You'll most likely observe greater focus and other improvements. My own experience and reports from clients suggest that the effects can be very powerful. The following is an example of how I apply these ideas in my own life.

One morning I was up before my family, contemplating the overwhelming number of commitments I had. The following day I had to travel. Before doing so, I had a number of technical and logistical problems to solve and errands to run, plus an almost packed day of social commitments. And this didn't even include preparing for the professional commitment I was traveling for. I was about to put my nose to the grindstone and start plowing through it all when a growing sense of panic and an impending headache made me reconsider.

I had serious problems to solve that would require a high level of organization and prioritization. The impulse to plow ahead had gotten me into trouble before. An image flashed through my mind: my family waking up to a mom frazzled and scattered, ready to start yelling at the smallest provocation. This was likely to become a reality if I just started to plow through my to-do list.

I had come to understand that nature and movement serve as medication for my ADD. For maximal effectiveness on that day, I needed to take my medication. I headed for the hills—literally. Even though it would take an hour and a half out of my already crowded day, I knew that the time I spent moving in nature would allow me to focus more clearly and perform with the high level of organization required. For a person without ADD, this activity in nature could have been a method of procrastination. For me, or any person with ADD, activity in nature is the prerequisite for effective, high-level functioning. Just as many people take their need for medication seriously, I take my need to get into nature and get moving seriously. It works, every time.

I returned with a clear head, gratified by the reminder that my husband could indeed manage to feed the kids breakfast. Other than the fact that my daughter sported a set of ponytails that made her look like a unicorn (one coming out the front of her head, the other from the back), the family had had a calm breakfast without me.

Taking the time to "medicate" yourself with nature often requires you to make choices. No matter how busy and hectic your life, realize that your effectiveness depends on your time in nature. If I had forced myself to plunge ahead—or had convinced myself that my kids would starve if I took the time to be in nature—I would have been headed for a day of irritability and low-level problem solving. Unfortunately, it can be hard to choose nature when no one validates your need for it. Our culture has become so fast paced and technology driven that a back-to-nature movement seems quaint at best. However, as noted before, my experience and observation suggest otherwise—nature is indeed potent medicine. Take this chapter as permission to give yourself the nature fix your brain and body crave.

My husband looks at me with disbelief when I put on my hiking shoes and say I'm off to work. It is while moving in nature that I write my books and do my best thinking about how to heal clients and how to understand their lives, gifts, and problems. It is also by moving in nature that I fill my own well. It is only from that place of fullness that I have anything to offer my family, friends, and clients. I see my time in nature not as a distraction or procrastination but as a fundamental ingredient of my work, healing, and personal fulfillment.

ACTIVITY: ACT LIKE A SCIENTIST

Many of my clients with ADD have found that being in nature dramatically increases their focusing power. One person told me that if she could spend one hour in nature in every day, her whole life would change. If, like this person, you know spending time in nature could heal you and your life but can't imagine how to find the time, try it as an experiment: don't make a long-term commitment, just act like a scientist and see what you discover.

1. The first step is to gather data. Starting on a Saturday, give yourself a full hour in nature first thing in the morning. (You may have to wake up an hour earlier than usual to do so.) Observe how the rest of your day unfolds. On Sunday, follow your regular schedule. Take notes on how nature did or did not impact your life and schedule. Note your ability to focus, your mood, your tension, and your level of organization. Compare Saturday and Sunday. Are there any differences?

2. The second step is to gather even more data. Any scientist knows that a small sample can produce misleading results because other factors may interfere. Other events or factors may have interfered with the effects of being in nature. For example, if a stressful event also occurred, you may not notice the full positive effects of your time spent in nature; similarly, if your experiment coincided with a celebration, you may tend to overestimate its positive mood benefits. Regardless of whether you got positive results or negative results from the first step, give yourself one hour in nature every day for one week. Continue to observe your focus, mood, tension, and level of organization. A week will give you the time to note any behavioral or performance changes. Questions to ask yourself include the following:

- Am I getting more or less work done?

- Am I able to identify priorities so as to better organize my commitments?

- Have I changed my ideas of which tasks are priorities and which are not?

- Have I gotten any big ideas that have created new energy or increased the likelihood of success in completing projects?

- Am I more or less stressed overall?

- Is one hour spent in nature daily a good investment or just procrastination?

3. Once you've collected this further data, review the results. Is adding time in nature healing for you? If you get positive results but you still wonder about the time investment, experiment with different amounts of time. Try a half hour and see what kind of results you get. Experiment, too, with how you spend your time in nature. If you've been lying on a blanket or lounge chair, see if walking or being physically active makes a difference. If you've been walking in your neighborhood, try a short drive to a more inspiring natural area. Many people find that, as with finding the right dosage of medication,

finding the right time, place, and level of activity for being in nature is important. These are all aspects that can be tweaked to great effect.

Damon: The Dolphin Whisperer

> *Over forty-five pounds of debris and garbage collected! Twenty-seven bags of garbage, plus eleven bags of recyclables, including glass bottles and aluminum cans. Many spent long hours under the hot sun. The temperature was at 90 degrees at nine a.m. We had cases of cold water ready and waiting for the volunteers. Please keep in mind, folks, that what you throw away at the beach hurts and can even kill the environment. This was part of the International Coastal Cleanup, with the Ocean Conservancy Works and Sarasota County.*

This was Damon Harper's summary of the beach cleanup he arranged. Damon Harper is a physical trainer and life coach who does most of his training on the beach or in the water. He describes his physical activity and connection to nature as both part of his personal therapy for ADD and how he helps his clients. His passion and purpose reveal the gift of ecological consciousness embedded in ADD. Damon contacted me regarding my book *The Gift of ADHD;* we corresponded by e-mail for a year and spoke in a series of phone calls in July 2007 for this profile.

Damon was diagnosed with ADD at the age of six. "From early childhood I was energetic, happy, and just full of life. The medical field in the early seventies diagnosed this as minimal brain dysfunction or hyperkinesis." What Damon considered happy and energetic was considered by others to be hyperactivity and distractibility. His account points to the varied perception of "symptoms" and how adults and children may see them quite differently. He was on Ritalin for many years. He has continued to take the medication on and off since his diagnosis at age six.

Damon told me that he not only connects with nature, but that nature allows him to connect with himself. This personal experience with nature has led him to conduct his physical therapy and personal training sessions in the ocean. He explained that working in nature greatly helps his clients: "It has really made others 'wake up' to themselves. They come see me for physical training, but find they need so much more just to get back in touch with themselves." Damon argues that being out of nature leads us to become disconnected from ourselves; he tries to restore this connection in his work.

Interestingly, Damon attributes his environmental activism directly to his ADD. He enjoys nature so much and is so sensitive that he can see what those who are not connected to nature cannot. He not only sees the destruction and waste, he also sees what needs to be done to start to address these problems—and he does it. Even more controversially, he contends that the medication used to treat his ADD symptoms also makes his activism go away. Damon told me that when the medication takes effect, his compassion for nature evaporates and he just plain stops caring. Although he admits that not caring can have its benefits—"Sometimes it just feels like a relief to not care so much"—he doesn't like these changes and therefore struggles with whether to take medication or not.

The effect that Damon speaks of hasn't yet been documented scientifically (ADD researchers have yet to seriously study "environmental concern" as a potential medication side effect), but if valid, its implications are profound. If ADD involves a brain hardwired for greater sensitivity to the natural world and medications reduce this sensitivity, will the natural world suffer if ADD adults are medicated en masse? While highly speculative, Damon's story suggests that this is an arena worth investigating.

The opening quotation from Damon, especially his reminder "Please keep in mind, folks, that what you throw away at the beach hurts and can even kill the environment," illustrates not only his passion for protecting nature but his general bigheartedness. His conversation is filled with his concern for animals of all sorts. He speaks with affection of the squirrels, bats, rats, and raccoons that he leaves food out for. He has launched many animal rescue missions, personally rescuing animals himself; recent rescues have included a bird with a broken wing, a squirrel, and a turtle.

For Damon, connecting to nature leads to healing and peak experiences. "I sense it I'm in it. The real magic is to allow whole body to be in reverence and appreciation of it." When he's in the ocean, he feels in greater control of his senses and more centered. He makes it a habit to visit the state parks in his home state of Florida often, but is frustrated by many of the people he encounters in such natural settings. "Other people don't respect nature, they're loud or they litter. I've always found that pokes a nerve with me. These are natural wildlife parks, but people don't respect them."

What's ADD Got to Do with It?

You may be wondering how ADD leads to a connection with nature. Part of the answer lies in the fundamental attentional stance of the ADD adult. For an ADD adult, attention is not focused like a laser. Rather, it is distributed and dispersed. The ADD adult's attention stretches far and wide, open to connections with all that it touches. Imagine steam evaporating from a pot of boiling water. The steam's openness allows it to mingle with other air particles, thus becoming entangled with other elements. So too does the ADD adult's attention merge with and have a tendency to feel connected to what it perceives. A laserlike attention doesn't mix with what it attends to, it points to it. Because ADD attention is so diffuse, it often mixes with what it attends to instead. This makes it harder to focus, but easier to experience empathy, compassion, and concern.

Damon recounted with excitement several vivid memories of directly connecting with wildlife. "One time I was at a park and there was a mama alligator seven feet away, resting in her nest. I don't know how I knew, but I knew she'd be okay if I came close to her." Damon sat within three feet of the alligator; he felt connected with her. She merely moved her tail and watched him. Although it scared his friend out of his wits, Damon sensed that he would be safe. Around snakes, too, he feels no fear. He spoke with affection of a big black snake that lives in his yard and told me, "I'll wash my clothes and snakes will get close. Don't mean any harm and doesn't harm me."

The Dolphin Whisperer

Damon speaks casually about his ability to understand marine life; he loves to go into the ocean at dusk, to be surrounded by dolphins and manatees. Once, when he was conducting a physical training session in the ocean, he saw a dolphin flapping its fin on the water and sensed that the dolphin was protecting him and his client for some reason. A few minutes later Damon saw a mother manatee and her calf only fifty feet away. Damon understood immediately that the dolphin was warning him to let the protective mother and her calf pass.

Ocean Therapy

Like many ADD adults, Damon is very creative. He invented a new form of physical and spiritual healing, called Ocean Therapy, and his business, Soul Strength Productions (www.DrSporty.com), honors his unique, creative brand of coaching and physical training.

Damon brings his clients into the ocean, where they do a combination of physical training, aerobics, tai chi, and relaxation techniques. He explained that many people who come for physical fitness are so transformed by their experience that they experience a realignment with their deeper values and purpose. "I don't do anything; I'm just there assisting—the ocean does the healing." The paradox is that many go to him to gain greater control, but the ocean offers them the experience of letting go of control and, as a result, they are able to connect with parts of themselves they had previously shoved to the side. He spoke of executives beginning to weep as they relaxed into the water, nurtured and nourished by nature herself.

For both Damon's clients and himself nature heals. "It's a makeover for your soul, a healing process, a recovering process." We ourselves are part of nature—becoming disconnected from nature is thus a loss of ourselves. Nature is a synergistic system of interdependence; in such a system, an entanglement with oceans and wildlife can be a great gift. Unlike those with ADD, those who are overly focused may glide right by this important relationship with nature that Damon eloquently points to. Perhaps it is cutting off this crucial connection that is the true deficit disorder of our times.

CHAPTER 7

Interpersonal Intuition

High-level executives and gang leaders share an ability to tune in to others; recognize their strengths, needs, and motives; and then use these insights to motivate, recruit talent, and lead. Many adults with ADD have this gift of interpersonal intuition—a quality with important applications in any arena. This intuitive grasp of what others need, feel, and want can be a great gift. Whether the CEO is searching for vulnerabilities in other companies and pressuring them to cave or the gang leader is studying the market to determine what deals to make with the cartels, these gifts can offer strategic advantages in many arenas. One woman with extensive experience working with ADD gang leaders believed that if her clients were to use their abilities for legal activities, they had the potential to become powerful community leaders. I've worked with CEOs and consulted with treatment providers for gang members; both groups have despaired of finding the gifts in ADD. This chapter will show you some of the directions in which I have guided individuals to help translate apparent deficits into gifts.

As an adult with ADD, you probably often blurt out inappropriate comments that get you in trouble.

You're often charged with having inappropriate boundaries and engaging in impulsive behavior. You're distracted when you talk to friends, family, and lovers. People complain you never seem to listen. Underlying these problems is a great gift: the ability to read others like a book. While high-level executives, entertainers, therapists, and artists with ADD have figured out how to tap into this great resource, for some adults with ADD, this gift has led to problems.

Because you tune in to other people on a deep level, you often dismiss their words outright. To make matters worse, when you share your impressions with others, you typically receive a swift, harsh denial that what you are saying could be true. Many adults with ADD have gone through their lives having their observations constantly denied. This is because you see things that others either want to hide or don't even see themselves.

In many ways, adults with ADD organically do the work of psychotherapists. Psychoanalytic therapists are trained to "listen with the third ear" (Reik 1948), meaning to use their own inner experience as a guide to the unconscious of a client. For example, if a therapist becomes distracted by an inner fantasy, she will study that fantasy as a reflection of the client's unconscious. Therapists use their inner worlds as guidance for understanding what a client is *not* saying.

The rule of thumb here is that a therapist's distraction is providing her with information about what is going on for the client. I have learned to trust my fantasies, to step back and shift between following a fantasy and scrutinizing it for relevance to my client's issue. For example, if I become bored during therapy, I take that as information that the client is not talking about his key issues. On one occasion I was distracted by a fantasy of Jim Carrey, the comic actor. I let my mind wander. I remembered an interview with him I'd seen on TV in which he said he suffered from depression, that unless he was far over the top every minute he felt worthless. He only felt good enough when he was jumping off the couch in wild antics, making hilarious faces with voice inflections to match. As I followed this fantasy I began to wonder if my client—whose main complaint was exhaustion—similarly pressured himself to mesmerize others with his antics. Thus, my "distraction" led me to a deeper understanding of both my client and the underlying dynamic of our therapy sessions, as even during these he felt a need to entertain.

While therapists use this intuitive ability strategically, many ADD adults tune in to others' inner worlds and unspoken emotions without knowing what they are doing or how to handle it. Psychologists have studied this process of finding deeper meanings in distraction; such work offers useful insights for ADD adults driven batty by this ability.

Theodor Reik, psychoanalyst and author of *Listening with the Third Ear* (1948), advises therapists in training to adopt an unattached, free-floating attention in order "to seize the secret messages that go from one unconscious to another" (145). Indeed, Reik defines focused attention as a blocking out of stimuli. To stay focused you need to cut off parts of your perception. Attention means you determine what is important and what is not and you give whatever you've determined important greater weight when you take in experiences. To focus is to actively cut out anything deemed unimportant. The difference then, is that when you're attending but not focusing you still take in the unimportant, you just don't give it as much of your energy.

Reik points out that when it's a case of understanding another person, we often won't know in advance what is important and what is not. More often than not, focused attention can thus actually cause us to misunderstand other people. Because our ideas about what is important are guided by our prejudices and preconceptions, approaching situations with focused attention will prevent us from gathering deep but unexpected information; rather, we will take in only that "important" information we are already looking to find.

Approaching relationships with focused attention similarly leads to finding whatever you are looking for. If you are talking to a person you think is smart and confident, you will focus your attention on words or traits that confirm this idea. If, on the other hand, your attention is free-floating, you will notice data a focused person would not. For example, you might notice that this know-it-all is desperate to please everyone, and realize that she must be insecure. In this way people with ADD—who don't direct their attention with expectations—can get a better read on others than more focused people. The ability to block out unimportant stimuli can serve a person well in any situation in which what is important is clearly defined, like in a classroom. But this very same ability will disable a person in situations like interpersonal ones, in which what is important isn't immediately clear.

Reik not only prescribes free-floating attention as a tool for therapists to understand clients, he also notes that when clients complain of attention difficulties, these difficulties are often caused by an openness to either their own unconscious or another's. He writes, "We often hear patients complain that they fail to concentrate their attention. In analytic investigation we find that this complaint conceals a totally different situation. The attention of these patients is concentrated, though, upon an unconscious content, for instance, certain fantasies" (169). He rightly points out that it is only the demands of the external situation that the client is not paying attention to. It is impossible for someone to actually "not be paying attention." In reality, while we are awake, we are paying attention, all the time.

Attention deficit disorder means only that we are not paying attention to what we are "supposed" to be paying attention to, as defined by the demands of a situation. Reik suggests that a distracted attention may actually indicate that a person is tuned in to either his own unconscious or another's. This type of connection to another's unconscious can lead to interpersonal insight. Adults with ADD are walking therapists, articulating deep and penetrating insights gleaned from the deepest recesses of another's mind—a great gift, but one that can easily get you into trouble with those who aren't looking for free therapy.

The problem is that, unlike therapists, adults with ADD aren't trained in understanding and using this stream of fantasy and impression that reflects the inner worlds of others. Instead, the ADD adult often experiences these fantasies and impressions as a flood of distractions that she can't make sense of. As a result, they can get her in trouble as easily as they can give her breakthrough insights.

It may surprise you that after being invalidated for so many years, your gift to see what's hidden still persists. If you've learned to dismiss it yourself, you've probably gotten into trouble with people you intuitively knew were shady or unreliable. It's time to stop dismissing your gift. ADD adults may be impulsive, but their quick reads of people reveal much that others miss.

UNREACHABLE

One possible downside to this quick read on others is that, as a result, ADD adults can be perceived by others as unreachable. You can use your insights as a barrier. Sometimes the constant invalidation can separate you from those whom you see all too clearly. It's hard to connect with someone who keeps telling you that you aren't seeing what you know you *are* seeing. Additionally, because you so keenly perceive what others try to hide, you may yourself use the information you gain as an excuse not to connect. You may assume that the people you would otherwise connect with are phonies.

The crux is that what you are seeing is often correct, at least in part. The phoniness you see is probably there. In many cases, this perception of phoniness can be a great gift. It can help you heal someone through revealing areas of inauthenticity, if your role is to do that. It can help you avoid situations that would lead to trouble. It can help you in business, sales, management, or marketing. It can help you hit the right note as an artist, or give you a target for your artistic expression. The key to embracing your ability to determine phoniness without falling prey to its negative side is to balance your discrimination with compassion. For example, when large stakes are on the table, it's important to use your discrimination and stay away from a person whom you feel you cannot trust. However, if you are on a date, it might be better to let yourself feel compassion for a person who is acting phony out of insecurity, perhaps giving the individual a second chance to see if the phoniness was actually just the influence of first-date anxiety. And even in cases when you do decide to cut involvement with a person, you can do so with compassion.

FLY-BY-NIGHT

Repeatedly having your perceptions invalidated can cause poor social judgment. It may be that so many people have told you that you're off base or just plain crazy that you've stopped trusting your insights. If this is the case, you're like a plane flying at night without a guidance system. Ironically, it may actually be that having shut off your intuition is what's causing so many problems in your personal and professional relationships. Being willing to take risks and defy expectations is a tremendous gift when paired with a sensitive intuition. But take away the guidance of that intuition and you have foolhardiness on speed—or just plain Ritalin.

CORE DESIRE

Focusing too much on where and when others are phonies can alienate you, preventing you from bonding with others. The irony is that underlying this alienation is a great ability and desire to connect. In some ways you see others so clearly because you connect very easily with them. You are like a pioneer in intimacy, forging new depths where others are content with more superficial stopping points. You reveal thoughts, emotions, delights, and concerns openly—and make others comfortable doing the same with you. You read others so well both because you can and because you want to. However, when your insights are consistently invalidated or you lack skill in handling your ability, you may lose sight of your core desire to connect.

A key strategy for turning this around is simply to remind yourself of your ability, need, and desire to connect deeply with others. In some ways, the reason you see phoniness in others is because you see so deeply. Like a sonar instrument reading the depths, your strong interpersonal intuition goes deep, thus increasing your chances of finding what others might choose not to reveal. If you can keep your desire to connect in mind, this gift can be used to heal relationships, not just as an excuse for leaving them.

INTIMACY PIONEER

You can go deeper than others. You can connect at levels others shy away from. As a result, as with any person forging uncharted territory, you are likely to discover impassable terrain. As you seek to connect more deeply, you will come upon places where others have slammed doors shut. It is your tendency to try to open these doors that makes others say you are "irreverent" and "rebellious" and "push buttons." Remember, there are often long-standing reasons for why others don't want to open these doors.

Merging Rather Than Managing

Whereas some people, keen on social hierarchies and appearances, manage relationships, you instead merge with the core of people you connect with. You search for a person's heart and will only be satisfied by finding the "real thing" in yourself and others.

One of your gifts is the capacity, courage, and desire to go as far as you can in connecting with others. You respond with eagerness to people you resonate with, regardless of their social desirability. Your intense curiosity can lead you to delve deeply into who the other person really is, rather than make judgments based on superficial traits.

The literature on psychotherapy offers descriptions similar to what ADD adults do naturally without recognizing what they are doing. The authors of *A General Theory of Love* (Lewis, Amini, and Lannon 2000) explain that therapists tune in to the emotions of clients by joining the client in a way that goes farther than just listening: "An attuned therapist ... doesn't just hear about an emotional life—the two of them live it. The gravitational tug of this patient's emotional world draws him away from his own, just as it should ... A therapist loosens his grip on his world and drifts, eyes open into whatever relationship the patient has in mind—even a connection so dark that it touches the worst in him. When he stays outside the other's world, he cannot affect it ... He takes up temporary residence in another's world ... Therapy becomes the ultimate inside job" (Lewis, Amini, and Lannon 2000, 178).

While therapists are trained to use this process of feeling with another as a tool for healing, the ADD adult may not be able to handle the feelings this leads to—or even recognize these feelings as belonging to others. But because you can resonate with others' feelings, you are also capable of merging with others. And because you can merge with others in this way, you also can read authenticity more easily than others.

It may be that others are less courageous than you. ADD adults will chase down any question or trace of insincerity in themselves. I've seen ADD adults consider turning down enviable opportunities because they think their motives may be tainted. In one case, a client was tormented by the idea that he might be taking a powerful position just to prove something to someone else. He decided that if he uncovered such a tainted motivation, he would not take the position. He eventually determined that his success was in alignment with his integrity and was able to move forward. His devotion to rooting out the insincere and false was admirable. If you recognize this quality in yourself, you probably see it as "the way things should be" rather than as admirable. And this is the sticky wicket for most ADD adults. Many—or even most—people are so focused on fulfilling expectations that they do not turn inward to see if their decisions ring with authenticity. An ADD person is not focused on others' expectations. This is a "symptom" of ADD, and also, from another light, a great gift.

The problem is that you may expect others to hold themselves to the same high standards of genuineness. You may repeatedly bump up against disappointment. I have heard ADD adults repeatedly rail against the consequences of failing to consider how important politics are in a system. Although you may expect your keen insights to be appreciated by others, they may actually create political tensions instead. The key to connecting is to imagine what it would feel like to be on the receiving end of your searing perceptions.

Rather than pointing out the missteps of those you are connected with, learn to see others with compassion. Use your insights in the service of your desire to connect. This will take some skill.

SKILLFUL MEANS

How do you honor your own keen perception and still connect with others sincerely? Start by realizing that every time you see something and say it without reflection (for example, "You need a beer" in a substance treatment center), your comments have a decent chance of either hurting someone's feelings or pushing a button she doesn't want pushed. Learn to insert reflection between your insight and the way in which you share it with others. Practice pausing before sharing any insight. Think of the possible consequences of hurting someone else. It may help to think of the word "incisive," as it captures both the incredible promise and the peril of this gift. According to Webster's (1996), incisive means "remarkably clear and direct; sharp; keen; and acute." This is a perfect description of this ADD gift: ADD adults see reality clearly and say it directly. However, incisive also means "cutting, biting, piercing"—even though clear and direct, your insights can be painful to someone who hasn't asked for them. When you pause before blurting out an insight, you gain time for perspective. With the pause, remind yourself how important timing can be in sharing your insights effectively. Opening up communication is a good thing; doing so with finesse is even better.

I have to admit that I enjoy the company of ADD adults, whose moment-by-moment "color commentary" can be like free therapy for the open-minded. Once, when my brother (who also has ADD) was exasperated with my reflections on the meaning of life, he burst out, "You have too much meaning in your life." At first his comment cut, but then I realized he had nailed it. As with any working parent, my life was already filled with too much; there was no void I needed to fill. My existential angst, which had previously served me well, had become nothing more than a bad habit. ADD clients often similarly turn the tables on me in therapy, accurately picking up unspoken tensions and barriers to connection.

As much as I, as an ADD adult myself, get a kick out of outbursts of inspired intuition, most people don't. Indeed, these kinds of outbursts can get ADD adults into a lot of trouble in personal relationships and work situations. The rub for you may be that you honor integrity so much that if you don't voice your perceptions, you can feel as if you yourself are becoming a phony. One way to handle this is to remember your intense need and desire to bond with others. If you can put that front and center, you can use your perceptions skillfully in the service of connection. Every time you have an insight about someone in your life, ask yourself the following questions:

- Will sharing this insight connect me more deeply with this person, or will it hurt our relationship?

- Will this insight empower me or disempower me if shared right now?

If you determine that sharing your insight won't connect you more deeply with this person, you may still need to do something with your insight. Like the prophet from the Old Testament who wrote that his injunctions felt like coals burning in his belly if he didn't speak them, you may feel physically or psychologically uncomfortable if you don't articulate the insights popping into your mind and heart. If so, try the following activity.

ACTIVITY: TURN ON YOUR HEART LIGHT

One particular impulse may often cause you to use your intuition in ways that create problems: the impulse to honor your integrity and to tell the truth. Let's address this impulse directly.

1. Ask yourself, "How can I both honor my keen insight and yet still forge a deep connection with this person?" Look for ways to break out of either-or

thinking. For example, it's easy to fall into the trap of thinking things like "Jane is selfish and manipulative, and in order for me to not be a phony I have to tell her what I see." Challenge this thought with flexible thinking. How can you honor your insight and still connect with the person? Write down as many answers as you can. For example, you might honor your integrity by setting clear limits and staying connected only in areas where the other person cannot manipulate you. (For example, "Sure we can golf together on weekends—when it fits into my schedule—but no more hooking me into elaborate plans to get out of work to hit the course.")

2. Ask yourself, "Can I express my insight in a way that will offer the other person information without being judgmental or hurtful?" If your first reaction is that you can't, try viewing a person's failings as simply a lack of information or training. For example, if you perceive another person as a downer to be around, rather than tell him what a drag he is, find a way to share with him the impact of his negative focus on you and others. Try something like "While your refined tastes allow you to offer compelling critiques, sometimes we just like to have fun and let loose without thinking about how things could be better." In this way you both share information that can genuinely be of service and recognize an underlying talent.

It may also be appropriate to translate your observations into a "teaching point." As long as the individual in question isn't someone who wouldn't appreciate a teaching point—like a boss or a supervisor—you can translate your irritation into specific guidance for how she can improve. For example, if she's a slow, boring talker, it may be as simple as saying, "Sometimes you have to speak to the MTV generation. Keep it short and entertaining—think sound bytes." In this way you address your irritation, while articulating only useful guidance.

3. Ask yourself, "Can I turn my irritation into compassion?" In terms of anger and irritation, you may go from zero to sixty in one second flat, while others have the gift of a slow burn. Intensity and impulsiveness can be a gift in many settings, but in relationships, being able to insert compassion between irritation and foot-in-mouth can go a long way in preventing blowups. Practice translating your irritation into reasons to feel sorry for the other person. Of course, these aren't things to say out loud; use them mentally to interrupt your habit of spouting irreverent insights. Here are some examples for common situations:

- How small he must feel if he needs to dominate every conversation.

• It must be so exhausting to know it all, all the time.

• How dull it must be to go through life as a slow, boring talker.

• It must be constricting to go through life so tense.

• She'll miss all the fun with her obsession with detail.

Similar ideas were presented in chapter 3 to help you improve your listening skills; now use them to translate your intuitive insights into compassion.

4. Not all of your insights are helpful all of the time. Ask yourself, "Rather than voice this insight, can I simply file it away as an observation on human nature?" Often the reason you blurt out an insight comes from an urge to connect. You feel that being with someone with integrity means sharing your insights. Remember that in the service of a greater goal (another relationship, a project that will serve many others), you may need to refrain from sharing your impressions. For example, if your insights about a relative of someone you love will hurt your connection with your beloved, you don't have to reveal them. Or, your role in a

time-limited project may call for you to simply do a job and move on, rather than forge a connection.

5. Anything you can insert between your irritation and free-form self-expression can prevent problems. The sillier, more vivid the interruption, the more easily you will be able to recall it. Sing the song "Turn On Your Heart Light" any time you find your irritation climbing and impatience taking over. Watch the movie *E.T.* so you'll have vivid images of a heart light and the importance of seeing with compassion. Download the song into your iPod. Sear this cheesy Neil Diamond tune into your mind to save you from emotional outbursts. If this isn't your style, find some other silly song or image to put between your irritation and a possible outburst. Any cue that will remind you to translate your irritation into compassion will work.

VISIONARY SOULS

ADD adults are forces for change. Many or most other people come into a situation trying to read others' expectations in order to conform to them. You come in wanting to shake things up, often with a vision of possibilities. However, the forces that resist change are very strong. Indeed, the dramatic conflicts you experience in relationships and work situations often occur when your innovative impulse meets these forces of resistance. It's hard to see something others really don't see. Because others may be focused on what they are supposed to do, they may not see hidden truths or unrealized possibilities. And because others may be afraid of change, they may be motivated not to see your visions. It can be hard to embrace change when resistance to change is almost a fundamental law of human behavior and organization.

For a person with a lifetime of being dismissed for dwelling in possibilities rather than real-world details—a person loaded with low self-esteem and confused about what is real—the situation is that much worse. Your intuitive inspirations are self-evident to you, yet meet with criticism at every turn. A lifetime of denials, starting with when you asked why Daddy was always mad and were told to shut up and proceeding from there, can make you feel pretty crazy. And a lifetime of not being heard can lead you to intense outbursts—as if by making a scene someone will have to take you seriously. Getting in trouble for making scenes will then lead to deeper humiliation and embarrassment. Add in the fear that you'll never get it right, and your emotional intensity will spiral out of control, making you that much less able to focus and concentrate. This will then lead you to lose track of your stuff, your ideas, your projects, and any details—giving others valid cause for complaint. Thus, the impact of having your intuition denied repeatedly can itself lead to emotional outbursts and massive disorganization.

If you can recognize this confusion about why your intuitions are repeatedly dismissed and the real-world reasons for it, you will have taken a step toward healing. The self-doubt you carry with you into your relationships and work life can actually cause more damage than your lack of interest in organization and details. Most teams, leaders, and people you love are willing to understand that your sharp ability to read people and situations can be a great contribution. But if you have a backlog of self-doubt, you come with a hair-trigger temper, ready to tell anyone who doubts you exactly where to go. To protect your natural gifts and give them the chance they need to gain credibility, you must first deal with your history of having your intuitions dismissed.

ACTIVITY: BACK TO THE PAST

What is your track record, really? It's time for you to unpack your heavy burden of having your interpersonal intuitions discredited. Often it takes the perspective of time to figure out when you were right and when you were off base—and to figure out, too, what you were really tapping into when you were off base. In this activity you will review memories of both when your insights were denied and you were right, and when your instincts were denied and you were wrong.

You will be asked to consider why you were wrong on these occasions. Often there are predictable reasons for being wrong. For example, if you're interacting with someone driven by a negative desire, you're likely to misread the situation. A *negative desire* is a strong wish for a specific outcome, motivated by an inauthentic force (for example, revenge or a need to prove yourself). This is one of the forces most likely to distort your natural gift for reading others. You will want to search for these possibilities.

1. In your journal, make a list of times when you read a situation perfectly and it served you well. For example, maybe you wanted to recruit someone to a cause of yours and you not only pegged the perfect person, you knew exactly what buttons to push to get him on board. This worked out well for you, for the person you recruited, and for the cause he joined. A win-win-win situation for all involved—one that would never have happened if not for your intuition skills.

2. Make a list of times when you had strong impressions that turned out to be wrong. From this list, select the three events that are the most vivid or

painful to you. For each event, first ask yourself if it's possible that you were right even though it seemed you were wrong. Consider the following ways in which you may have been right even when it seemed you were wrong:

• You may have read one or more people on a team correctly but didn't take into account group dynamics, particularly if the information involved a group decision.

• You may have correctly read the unconscious of a person, which she herself may have never gained awareness of.

• You may have read the situation at hand correctly, but real-world forces were in play that were not on your radar screen.

• You may have been right about a person's feelings for you but didn't realize that the feelings were not personal or unique toward you—for example, a lady killer's attraction to you, or a pessimist's low evaluation of you. In this case, you are reading the person correctly, but what you see isn't a truth in specific relation to you but simply the generalized style of the person whom you are reading.

There are many ways to correctly read a person and situation and yet be wrong about the events that actually play out. Generate your own reasons for why you may have actually been right. Generate as many reasons as you can for why your intuition may have been right, while the outcome you expected was wrong.

3. Now look at your list of three events again. This time, consider that you may have been wrong. Ask yourself the following questions:

• Was I influenced by wanting a specific outcome that was out of alignment with my own deepest interests? (For example, were you fooling yourself that you wanted to settle down and have kids when really you just wanted to roam the world, and thus, because you knew all along it wouldn't last, read your partner's level of involvement wrong?)

• Was I missing specific concrete information that would have helped me interpret the vibes I was getting? As a psychologist, I have the opportunity to test my intuition regularly in a context where I can easily ask for immediate feedback. I've found that when my intuition misses the mark, it's often because there are specific facts, areas of expertise, and contexts I'm simply not aware of.

• Is there a deeper reason for being wrong? Don Quixote is iconic for mistaking windmills for dragons to be slain, but this very error provided the fuel for grand adventures and endless entertainment. Consider whether your mistake led you to explore previously unfamiliar areas or become something you might not have otherwise been. Many people wonder why they read others as more romantically interested than they are. Sometimes these doomed involvements lead to the realization of your own capacity for love—or even just to new interests.

4. Now, make a list of times when your intuitions were spot-on correct and this led to negative consequences. This outcome—a correct intuition leading to negative consequences—can cause you to turn off your own intuitive guidance and leave you with a poor ability to express yourself skillfully. Being wrong is easy compared to being right and messing up your life as a result. A mess-up might be as major as losing a meaningful relationship because you shared insights the other person didn't want to hear, or as awkward as becoming aware of a secret extramarital affair a close friend is having.

HOW TO LET GO

As an ADD adult, you have the ability to almost channel what other people are thinking and feeling.

Typically you are profoundly emotionally engaged and read others exceptionally well. You connect intuitively with others—often anticipating what they are about to say—and are highly attuned to interpersonal dynamics. Indeed, you may even find yourself feeling what the other person feels.

This entanglement with others can make it very difficult for you to let go once you connect. Letting go can be even more difficult because those you have connected with have passed through your BS detector and stayed with you, even though you may have thrown into their faces all the defenses, phoniness, and barriers you sounded out. One of the traps ADD adults frequently fall into is taking the interpersonal connection too far and not letting go when the other person is not connected at the same level. Sometimes ADD adults feel they know another person better than the other person knows himself. Although this may be true at some level, it doesn't mean the other person will be motivated to connect.

For this reason, ADD adults need to learn to grieve and let go. One of the most important steps in letting go is giving yourself permission to be wherever you are in your grief. For example, you may feel that you don't want to let go. That's okay. If so, be fully present in not wanting to let go. Don't try to jump over wherever you are now to get to the stage of being able to let go—it won't work.

Whatever stage you are at, give yourself full permission to go deeply into that stage. The following is a list of statements that may represent where you are in relation to letting go. Let yourself feel these statements and be wherever you are for as long as you need. Say to yourself, "I can be sad as much as I want, for as long as I want. I can be mad as much as I want, for as long as I want. I can be afraid as much as I want, for as long as I want." Apply this to wherever you are now in the grief process. The fundamental life skill lacking in today's culture is the ability to let go. The following reflections will resonate with different stages in the process of letting go. Circle the statements that resonate with wherever you are now:

- I can't let go of you.
- I don't know how to let go of you.
- I can't believe you are not part of my future.
- What we shared was one of the most meaningful relationships in my life.
- You not being in my future doesn't take away the luminous moments we shared.
- I will still take you with me into my future through who I have become because of you.

- I cry and let the waves of grief overcome me.
- I wish you were part of my present and future ... but you are not.
- It's okay to keep wishing you were here with me.
- You are part of the rich tapestry of my soul and always will be, but I must let you go your own way now. I let you go, but I thank you for what we shared.
- I know you are not a part of my future, but it's okay for me to wish you were as long as I need to.
- It's okay for me to talk to you in my mind even though I have to let you go.
- It's okay for me to feel hurt as long as I need to.
- Maybe you rejected me because you were afraid of my love; still, I need to let you go.
- Even though you rejected me, I can still honor the love I feel for you.
- Letting go is hard; it's not supposed to be easy.

- I am often torn between releasing you and making desperate plans to get you back; I don't act on the plans, but I honor my wish to be close to you.

- I heal my emotional pain by taking good care of myself, identifying my needs, and taking care of them.

- I allow myself to trust that there is a greater purpose in loving and leaving you.

- I allow my heart to open by feeling this heartache.

- I will let my heart ache as long as it wants to.

- I don't want to lose what we had.

- I can't let go because I don't trust something new will come.

- I can't let go because I don't know who I am and where I am going.

- I'm about to make that leap from here to there—here being the life that derived some of its fullness from your presence, and there being the life in which you are a memory. I make the leap with deep sadness. I loved you.

Kim McCoy: Interpersonal Genius

For the first time ever, I eagerly anticipated the task of checking references. These references read like a who's who of eminent clinical psychologists. I was excited to chat with such luminaries about Kim McCoy, the woman I was thinking about hiring, and a very bright prospect indeed. Her pedigree included degrees from the finest clinical training institutions in the nation and work with notable advisors.

The position I was hiring for required deep gifts. My research assistant would be entering potentially inflammable situations and interacting with severely mentally ill clients prone to outbursts and inappropriate gestures at every turn. In addition, she would face the task of collecting research data in a clinical setting. She was likely to meet antagonism from clinical providers protective of their clients and skeptical of researchers. She would have to carefully navigate conflicts between clients and their case managers, whose approval was needed for participation in this study. To rigorously collect data from volatile clients, she would need to have enormous social graces and the highest level of clinical skills. And since Kim was an attractive young woman, she would almost certainly also have to contend with a steady stream of lewd gestures and comments from impaired clients. This milieu was filled with potential land mines. I needed someone who could handle it all with composure.

Every luminary on her reference list assured me Kim would easily be able to handle these enormous challenges. But each one felt compelled to include a "but": "But follow-through is a problem for her." "But she takes a long time to complete projects." "But she has difficulty focusing and following through." After some further discussion with each reference, I resolved to hire her.

It was Kim's interpersonal intuition that caused her to stand out amidst a pool of talented applicants in the first place. Hiring a research assistant in the San Francisco Bay Area, where some of the finest training institutions in the nation are located and there are lots of bright, eager students, is not an enviable task. I saw quickly that many of the applicants would have as much to offer me as I would offer them in supervision and training. As bright as they were, I was certain each would challenge me to think about the meaning of the study and the implications of its findings, as well as offer me insights into logistical snafus. Kim distinguished herself with one sentence: "I can see you need to finish your data collection and I'll work until you have finished your sample." She read my most urgent need and assured me that she could meet it. Every other applicant tried to impress me with over-the-top credentials. The problem was, *every* applicant was over the top in intelligence, training, and skills.

Kim's ability to quickly size up my most pressing need was uncanny. She was right: I needed a single person to complete the job. It wasn't just that if my assistant left partway through I'd have to train someone else; if the person I hired didn't complete the data collection, the quality of the data collected would be compromised—different raters from different backgrounds would add "noise" to the results, decreasing the data's reliability. It was this one sentence—demonstrating both her recognition of the essence of my problem and her willingness to solve it—that landed her the job. Even when her references offered their candid qualifications, her clarity about my situation overcame the concerns I had.

This vividly illustrates how intellectual gifts can interact with interpersonal gifts. Intellectual gifts lead to superiority in collecting, gathering, and evaluating information. Interpersonal gifts involve sizing up situations, attuning to specific motivations, identifying urgent needs, and offering convincing answers to these needs. It was here that Kim distinguished herself from those who were her equal in terms of intellectual accomplishments.

Over the course of my career, I have taught, supervised, or mentored hundreds of people. Most of these people I have admired greatly and felt honored to connect with. Only one of these people has become a personal friend—Kim. The transition from mentor-mentee to personal friendship is a tough one to make. These early roles can be an obstacle to equal friendship. For a true friendship to develop, the motivation has to be high. My immense respect for Kim's great gifts and her incomparable ability to connect propelled our relationship from a professional one to a personal one. The details included in this profile evolved out of both our ongoing personal relationship of more than eight years and a series of focused interviews in person and over the phone in the summer of 2007.

The Tables Turn

"It's okay for you to get tough with me, that's your job," Kim told me. We were reviewing some sloppy mistakes she had made. The mistakes were minor omissions, easy enough to correct, but requiring me to check her work and call her in order to get the missing information. In response, instead of becoming defensive or overly apologetic, Kim focused her energy on reading me—and once again provided the interpersonal guidance needed for our collaboration to work.

Kim's ability to navigate through complex roles and relationships to arrive at important interpersonal guidance was remarkable, and one I had never encountered so strongly. Indeed, in this particular case, I needed to get tough with her so she would be motivated to complete her work without omissions—and she needed me to be tough so she could trust that my feedback wouldn't be whitewashed by social pleasantries. She read me on two levels at once: she saw both my tendency to be nice and patch over potential conflicts and the seriousness of the correction that needed to be made despite my glossing over it. In addition, she was able to identify a simple behavioral step—getting tough with her—that I could take to extricate both of us from my difficulty with leadership. In effect, she became my leadership coach.

Kim not only filled my—at the time hidden—need for a leadership coach, her work in the clinic was unmatchable. I would easily have agreed to chase after data and omissions with her—which I had to continue to do—because I knew very well that I wouldn't be able to find anyone who would come close to meeting the competing demands she effortlessly fulfilled. The case managers who referred clients to our study were completely enamored of Kim. Often, researchers can seem threatening to health care providers. Researchers can make providers fear that their skills are being rated and their clients exploited. Kim, however, immediately relieved each care provider of any and all concerns. She connected individually with providers; Kim read their concerns, and—just as she had with me—said precisely the right words to convince them that their clients were in caring and capable hands.

Not only did she not rebuff the care providers—a mistake other researchers had made in this same setting—she won their admiration and respect. I repeatedly received unsolicited comments from care providers about her grace and skill. Even more impressive than her wooing of the care providers was her ability to win the trust of study clients—individuals who were severely mentally ill and distrustful at best and paranoid at worst. She often had to take in and meet the needs of both the care provider and the client at the same time.

On one occasion, a client in the midst of a manic episode was eager and insistent that she do the study right away. However, her case manager was concerned that the excitement of participating in the study would overstimulate this client, making her manic episode that much worse. Kim accurately read the conflicting needs and concerns of both the client and the case manager and landed on a brilliant resolution: she would allow the client to "practice" on the computer for a few minutes, and then would schedule a time at a later date when she could come in and complete the study. The data collection process involved giving the clients access to a computer and a brief tutorial so that they could answer questions in privacy. Kim went ahead and gave the manic client the tutorial and a few minutes to play around with the computer. In this way, she simultaneously won the trust of both the client and the case manager.

"The key to connecting is to be respectful of where the other person is and to never let them lose face," said Kim. She demonstrated respect for the client by honoring the client's needs, and respect for the case manager by showing that she, too, was protective of the client. Kim put aside her need to collect data and instead responded to the needs of both the client and the case manager. It was a delicate and demanding balancing act, but one that Kim pulled off with remarkable ease.

Going into the study we knew that other researchers had failed in this same setting. After the study, I asked Kim how she had succeeded where others had failed. She told me that the disparity between researchers' perspectives and these clients' perspectives was vast. "These clients were poor, uneducated, needy—people on the edge or already over the edge. I was able to meet them there with respect for their position and without a sense of entitlement because of my position." In reflecting on her role more broadly as a therapist, she said, "Too many therapists hijack therapy," by which she meant that, instead of resonating with a client's story, therapists sometimes try to co-opt it. In an effort to push for change, some therapists tell clients that their stories aren't as bad as they think, or that their needs aren't as pressing. Kim explained that intuition is a double-edged sword: "You have to use your own experience to resonate with another person, but you can't use your story to explain the other person's experience."

Kim's formula for connecting with others is simple: make your goal secondary to their goal. As part of our study, Kim had to sit at a desk in a treatment center and either persuade clients to sign up for the study or get case managers to refer their clients to it. While she was sitting there, she realized that many of the clients could practice the basic social skills they were learning from their case managers on her. She convinced case managers that the study would be a chance for clients to practice their basic skills and promised to give both client and case manager direct and clear feedback on how each client did and what the client might do to improve.

Although the case managers had been predisposed to think of researchers as exploiters of their clients, Kim's suggestion now effected a dramatic turnaround. Through Kim's ability to intuit interpersonal needs, the study came to be seen as a much-sought-after opportunity rather than an experiment using clients as guinea pigs. Kim achieved this not by pushing her need to collect data onto clients and case managers, but instead by intuiting and gathering information about what the clients and case managers needed.

Clients felt comfortable practicing with Kim because they could sense her nonjudgmental and open attitude. Because of their odd behavior and often unkempt appearance, severely mentally ill clients are frequently subjected to insults and injuries on a daily basis. Kim told me, "I always found something to like about everyone. Someone would come into the room, not having bathed in weeks. At first I would wonder how he could stand it, why he didn't take a shower or bath. But as soon as I started talking to him, he would have the wryest sense of humor, and start to make jokes. I always found each person interesting." Kim contrasted her approach to the "faux sympathy" of some other care providers—sympathy only in the sense of having pity for someone who is beneath you. Real sympathy involves caring without a sense of being one up. Kim attributes her ability to avoid faux sympathy to her personal struggle with ADD.

Her Own Shame

After being diagnosed with ADD, Kim struggled with enormous shame. She remembers feeling helpless when she was given the diagnosis. She felt vulnerable to others' evaluations. She felt like a round peg in a square hole (a phrase I've heard ADD adults use over and over to describe the course of their life). She also felt acutely ashamed of going to get help, of talking openly about her symptoms and her level of functioning.

From her own experience with shame—as a spiral leading to more helplessness and then even more shame—Kim realized that when people feel ashamed they stop learning and cooperating. She applied this understanding to the severely mentally ill clients participating in our study. As a result, she treated each study participant with great sensitivity and strove to create a collaborative environment, knowing that, like her, the participants probably felt deeply ashamed when talking about their symptoms.

In speaking about her intuition—an ability all of her supervisors had commended—Kim explained that when asked how she arrived at the right intervention at the right time, she usually had to reply, "It's just intuition. I just felt like it was the right thing to say." She speaks fondly of being supervised by the renowned psychologist Enrico Jones and his influence on her understanding of intuition.

Enrico Jones pushed Kim to explore how she actually arrived at her intuitive interventions. Kim became convinced that her intuition was the result of her unconscious expertise and patterns that she recognized but could not yet articulate. This understanding not only helped Kim to reflect deeply on her work, it encouraged her to try to consciously translate her intuition into specific patterns applied in new contexts.

Rules for the Road

My experience with Kim led me to develop a useful rule of thumb for supervising ADD adults. I'm often consulted by people who parent, supervise, or are married to individuals with ADD. I advise parents, bosses, and spouses to ask themselves whether the value of the individual's ADD gifts—gifts that include interpersonal intuition, exuberance, sensitivity, and creativity—outweighs the cost of addressing the individual's weaknesses. In many cases, the answer will be obvious. In the case of Kim, the effort it took me to double-check a few clerical errors was well worth the interpersonal genius she brought to the project—a project studded with some of the most complicated interpersonal land mines I have ever encountered.

CHAPTER 8

Translate Hyperactivity into Exuberance

One reason that adults are more likely to be labeled with ADD rather than ADHD is that the process of aging often takes some of the hyperactivity out of us. Many of my clients report that one positive side effect of aging is that it slows them down, making them more like other people in terms of tempo and their need for stimulation and activity. However, even clients who report this side effect are still noticeably different from others in their high level of energy. This hyperactivity can be translated into exuberance—a quality most of us admire with wonder.

Exuberance is a high-spirited liveliness; it's having lots of energy to follow passionate interests. Your intense curiosity may take you down pathways others would never find, may lead you on adventures or wild goose chases. You may talk at a hundred miles a minute or even faster. You may see those without ADD as "slow, boring talkers," as one adult with ADD called almost everyone else in the world. Your zest may make others' conversation seem to drone on endlessly. Your tendency to fidget constantly, wishing you could be set free from the constraints to sit still, may be an exuberance to express your energy and high spirits. You may prefer extreme sports, extreme vacations, extreme almost anything to structured activities. You may wish people would stop telling you to slow down and yearn for someone to instead match your speed.

To find the gift in your hyperactivity, you must first accept your desire for physical movement and stimulation as a need rather than a symptom. When you take this need seriously, your hyperactivity can fuel productivity and creativity. Having a high level of energy is one of the greatest gifts anyone can have; the older we get, the more obvious this becomes. When you give yourself permission to translate your hyperactivity into enthusiasm, you unleash the power to get your life on track and make dreams come true. It's time to get in touch with your wild child and let her out.

Hyperactivity is more than just moving and talking at fast speeds. Hyperactivity also includes an intense internal drive. The constant physical movements of hyperactivity correlate to being pushed and pulled by inner urgings, instincts, and promptings. In addition to high energy, hyperactivity is the quickness between an impulse and behavior. Where others without ADD extol the virtues of planning, the ADD adult moves quickly from impulse to real-world action. Others may see this as recklessness.

RECKLESSNESS

This recklessness can get ADD adults into trouble. When you embark on a wild scheme without pausing for reflection, you may cross a line or two you shouldn't. An example of such recklessness may be the ADD adult jumping off a cruise ship while it's in port just for the fun of it. While the downsides of recklessness are obvious, its negative consequences are probably exaggerated by the overly cautious. Recklessness is also the Wall Street suit telling off a major client for making foolish requests. When he discovers it was his firm's biggest client he cringes with regret—only to learn moments later that this client has requested that he be the only person who handles its orders. Some people recognize the value of being told how it really is. As often as recklessness leads to messes that need to be cleaned up, it also leads to opportunities.

Most therapists think of their role as helping clients make prudent, rational choices. I've been stupefied by the amazing results clients have achieved by making daredevil moves in their professional and personal choices. I've observed that when people want to achieve extraordinary things, they usually have to make extraordinary, reckless choices—choices that are frankly inadvisable.

The problem with psychotherapy is that it aims at making people normal. The bedrock assumption of many forms of both healing and education is that differences are disorders and that people should act in ways that will maintain stability. The problem with this is that if a person has original and dazzling contributions to make, she will act and think in ways that others would deem abnormal and reckless.

In my observation, successful ADD adults have typically been rewarded for their recklessness more often than they have been punished for it; as a result, they have learned to trust their instincts and plunge into action without any assurance of safety. If you always follow rules, you probably won't be a visionary leader. Leaders need both this sort of high energy and an inner capacity to create rules rather than just follow them.

The ADD adult's recklessness is often driven by the need to be doing, rather than planning or figuring something out. It's "Fire, ready, aim!" instead of "Ready, aim, fire!" This reversal of the normal order, this acting before planning, can be a highly effective way to gather information others will never have. If a course of action bears visible risks that others will not take but you will, you will learn things those others won't. You may fail more often, but in doing so gain valuable skills, contacts, and experiences.

Balls Out

Going "balls out" means being reckless in each moment and going for what you really desire, even if that changes frequently. By definition, recklessness is taking a course of action that would be generally inadvisable. For that reason, no self-help book, not even this one, would recommend that you seek out reckless activities. But recklessness will also set you apart from others. A course of action that few would take can bear the potential to achieve what few would achieve.

While recklessness is probably almost always a bad move for those who are employed by others, for those who are leaders, entrepreneurs, artists, or otherwise innovators, recklessness may be part and parcel of thriving. To go against what is advisable can be to create something original. If your recklessness pays off, you may find yourself a leader.

The important question is, what is your recklessness in the service of? If you are reckless in pursuit of desires in alignment with your sweet spot (see chapter 2), you may increase your chances of success. If you are reckless simply for the sake of a stimulation high, you may increase your chances of making foolish choices that lead to regret.

When recklessness is guided by a deep self-trust, it can lead to new vistas. Recklessness is the urge to act without any calculation of the costs and benefits of such action. If you have learned to trust your gut instincts, recklessness can be a daring expression of self-trust—it can be a sign that you give yourself permission to be the authority on your own life.

Recklessness requires a willingness to step into the unknown. You can only become more than you presently are by stepping out of where you are now. Indeed, recklessness may be an essential ingredient for growth and expansion. If you are to become who you are capable of being, you may have to let go of who you have been. It may be that it is only through recklessness that you can shed an outworn identity. For many, fear of the unknown leads to staying in bad relationships or bad jobs. Recklessness, then, may be a form of courage that frees people from fear, allowing them to move on and create a life they love.

Recklessness as Learning

Recklessness can be a source of real learning. When you act in ways others have not—indeed, in ways that others may have specifically urged you *not* to act—you gain experiences that others do not have. Each experience of unexplored territory can make you an expert in an arena where others are not.

Even if the only data you gather is from the process of failing, you will still have learned something others have not. Thus, each experience achieved through recklessness will make you an authority in a new arena. As a result, you will have experience, observations, and new instincts about what lies on the other side of expert guidance and accepted wisdom.

Trusting an urge, an impulse, or a wild idea will also develop your capacity for self-trust. You will either learn that your impulse was a good idea, or that you can bounce back from bad ideas. It's important to trust your own experience; if you do not, then on most occasions you will defer to the judgment of experts, setting up yourself to always be wrong and the expert to always be right. As a result, you will never learn anything in the very marrow of your bones. In defying the experts or advisable courses of action, you commit yourself to making a contribution. Without recklessness, you may dismiss your potential contributions because they are in conflict with mainstream norms.

ACTIVITY: INSPIRED IMPULSIVITY

When you channel your reckless impulsivity to serve your higher goals, it can be a force for making your dreams come true. (To remind yourself of your areas of passionate engagement, you may want to review chapter 2 and your answers to its Passionate Possibilities activity about finding your sweet spot.)

1. Write down three desires you have that fill you with a sense of passion and purpose.

[Space left intentionally blank in the original book]

2. Write down three courses of action that would be "reckless" but might make your dreams come true. (For example, if you wanted your marriage to be filled with passion, you could take off on a surprise vacation with your partner without any preparation or planning.)

[Space left intentionally blank in the original book]

3. Sometimes you may get lost in big plans and long-term goals and as a result overlook the guidance inherent in smaller, ever-changing desires and impulses. Write down three fleeting impulses you had in the last week.

[Space left intentionally blank in the original book]

4. How do these fleeting impulses relate to your bigger dreams and desires?

[Space left intentionally blank in the original book]

Sometimes destructive or addictive impulses actually conceal urges to pursue real dreams. Next time you feel a destructive impulse, replace it immediately with one of the "reckless" behaviors in the service of your purpose and passion that you identified in question 2.

HYPERACTIVITY AS DRIVEN DESIRE

One of the most common complaints of ADD adults is feeling driven by a motor. Indeed, this is why one popular ADD book is entitled *Driven to Distraction* (Hallowell and Ratey 1994). The bright side of this motor is that it gives you high levels of energy, keeping you energized long after others feel wiped out. The dark side is that this motor can be hard to turn off. Another problem with the exuberance of hyperactivity is that there is no "little general" to do the driving. Because there is no central organizing force behind the exuberance, your activity will often be scattered. You may be driven to finish a work project one moment, only to be distracted the next by the urge to phone a loved one—a call you never get to because as you pick up the phone you realize you're eager to get some recreation in. You're always on the move, changing directions moment by moment.

Whereas non-ADD adults can ignore their desires in order to get through a never-ending to-do list, ADD adults are vehemently connected to their desires. Almost every impulse that flits across their awareness seeks expression in the real world. The gift in this drive is that it helps you to recognize and honor your own needs. Your urges and wants *should* guide your life. And because you honor your desires so well, you have a full, healthy garden of desires, whereas others who are less exuberant have only a few scraggly, stunted weeds. These desires fuel your hyperactivity; they propel you with great energy to make them real.

The problem is, because immediate desires are so compelling, you may never become organized enough to work toward long-term goals. It's hard not to erupt into conversation when an idea flits across your mind—the short-term desire to share can be undeniable. It can take reflection to realize that your long-term goal of enjoying collegial relationships at work requires the ability to listen to others, even though they may seem slow, boring talkers.

Hyperactivity can be seen as a form of integrity. Integrity means honoring your sense of who you truly are and where you stand in the world. For ADD adults, an urge can be a powerful expression of their authentic self. When ADD adults do not act on their impulses, they can feel they are being phonies. In therapy, I help ADD adults manage this impulsiveness by putting a deeper, broader vision front and center—something that to honor they will have to restrain some of their most immediate urges. In this way, they realize that using restraint is in the service of their integrity, not a cop-out. For example, if a woman wants to fulfill long-range goals of marriage and family, rather than immediately indulging her impulse to have sex, she may want to move slowly in a relationship—especially if she's likely to regret the sex or feel burned by her romantic interest. If she can keep her long-term goals in mind, she can reframe integrity to mean acting to increase the likelihood of her deeper vision.

ACTIVITY: UNLEASH THE POWER OF YOUR CORE DESIRE

You probably often act in ways that are not in your best interest. You may fidget and try too hard to be entertaining when courting a romantic interest. You may talk too much and listen too little in strategic planning sessions, alienating others you want to connect to. Your hyperactivity can insist that you honor each and every impulse you feel. The flip side of this raw authenticity is that it may obstruct goals that require more time to achieve. As one improv instructor tells students, "Some guiding force underlies each moment. We need to keep in mind what we are aiming for. Instead of asking, 'What do I feel like doing?' substitute 'What is my purpose now?'" (Madson 2005, 84). This activity will help you align yourself with your most powerful guiding visions:

1. In your journal, record a recent experience in which you received negative feedback or didn't achieve the effect you hoped for because of your hyperactivity. For example, maybe you were too impatient to listen to a consultant you'd hired, and as a result wasted a lot of time and money.

2. Reflect on how your actions were motivated by a need to honor your inner experiences and live in your integrity.

3. Write out a broader, long-term goal that you did not achieve as a result of the experience recorded in step 1. For example, perhaps, because you didn't listen to the business consultant, you didn't increase your market and thus didn't reach your financial goals.

4. Translate this broader goal into a mission statement. Consider both concrete goals and any broader contributions you hope to make. Your mission statement could be as simple as "I want to keep my job to support my family" or as expansive as "I want to help heal the planet by distributing my artwork across the globe." Remember that once you are in touch with your grandest, deepest vision,

staying in your integrity may demand that you *don't* honor lower impulses (for example, you won't want to get mad at a person key to achieving your vision).

When you channel your exuberance into a mission statement, you unleash your motivation and self-control. One of the gifts of your ADD is that it makes you uncompromising in honoring your own instincts—a rarity in today's world, where many focus more on their image and the impression they make than on their integrity. The problem you have had up to now is that your enthusiasm has been untamed and shortsighted. You have not organized your desires and dreams, and as a result some of your big dreams have been hindered by smaller, less meaningful desires. This activity helps you to organize your desires, so that your integrity can be oriented around your deepest aspirations. This simple act of clarifying your most pressing dreams will help you honor your integrity and fulfill your greatest potential.

TRYING TOO HARD

Sometimes an ADD adult's hyperactivity is driven by what I call a "class-clown complex." Many ADD adults are recovering class clowns. Some ADD adults are still class clowns. If this is you, you can be funny, entertaining, and the life of the party. The problem is, if you have gotten used to the laughs, you may have come to need them. Perhaps the laughs absorb your hyperactivity in some way, dispersing your frenetic energy. Or the attention may be stimulation you crave. This applies to any form of attention. Getting attention from others may drive you to act so as to continue to receive this attention.

Your interpersonal intuition may also be telling you that other people expect you to be "larger than life." You may take your antics up a notch to live up to your reputation as "the spaz" or just plain fun to be around. Even if the attention you receive from others is negative, it can goad you to fulfill their expectations. In *The Gift of ADHD Activity Book* (2008), I discussed a convicted felon who described his criminal trial as one of the best times of his life because he received so much attention during it from so many people. Any attention you get for your hyperactivity may fuel you to take it to the next level.

One problem with trying to be larger than life is that, even though hyperactivity is an excess of energy, your efforts to entertain others may leave you exhausted and worn-out. Constantly trying so hard can sap you dry. A need to always be performing can paradoxically both make you the life of the party and give you an imposter complex because it leaves you so depleted inside.

I advise ADD adults who are stuck in this trap to give themselves permission to not try so hard. You don't have to live up to another's idea that you are fun to be around. Just be who you are. If you are an ADD adult, you probably think and act differently enough from others that you just don't need to try to get attention. Being with an ADD adult who feels the need to perform for others can be like going to a movie screened in high definition on the side of the Grand Canyon, with a full moon and a spectacular meteor shower raining down from above, and the band U2 playing a concert in the background. The point is that these distractions are exhausting for others as well as the ADD adult. You have much to offer without even trying—you don't need to add anything extra.

Trying too hard may be a holdover from your school days, when such antics were applauded. It can also be a holdover from efforts to compensate for not fitting in at school. If this is true for you, it's time to take a developmental leap: let yourself take a break.

ACTIVITY: TRY TOO LITTLE

Think of this activity as an experiment to observe what happens when you change your level of activity. If nothing else, you will learn that you can control how much you talk, act, entertain, ham it up, and perform.

1. Think of an area where you get into trouble either because you are too active or because others think you are over-the-top. This might be in relationships or professional settings. Write about a recent incident in your journal. (For example, John finds it so difficult to sit still at staff meetings that he tries to keep himself stimulated by raising his hand and talking all the time. He realizes, however, that others would probably prefer that he take more of a backseat role.)

2. Write out a "pregame" strategy for the next time you are in this situation. Plan to try too little, not too hard. For example, if you typically talk too much, your strategy might be listen first, talk second. You can even write it on an index card to take to the meeting with you. Spend some time thinking about what drives you to be so hyperactive and do some problem solving. For example, if it's your need for stimulation that causes you to talk instead of listening, you could doodle, play with a Koosh ball, or use some other tool to keep your hands moving while you listen.

3. Conduct a "postgame" review. How did not trying so hard affect the situation? Notice any differences. You may be amazed to realize how much you can learn when you stop talking, how much you can connect with a date when you are not trying so hard.

Write out any positive or negative reactions you had, as well as any feedback you received from others.

4. As you continue to practice taking your activity level down a notch or two, be gentle with yourself. If you go on a date with a pregame plan to be calmer but mess it up, know that just recognizing that you blew it is progress. Afterward, take the time to explore what went wrong and do some problem solving. Also, remember that sometimes it's just a matter of practice, practice, practice.

TIP OF THE ICEBERG

Different adults handle their hyperactivity differently. Whereas some naturally amp it up with class-clown antics, some ADD adults actually need to embrace their hyperactivity further. In my observation, this is more likely to be true for women with ADD who have learned to tame their hyperactivity, but it can also be true for men. If your hyperactivity was punished or rejected when you were a child, you may have developed strategies for denying it. Usually vestiges of it will still remain, however. One woman described a continuous need to fidget with the cap of her pen, often flicking it across the room. She acknowledged that she would like to be much more physically active throughout her day but didn't have the chance. Another woman—who experienced depression as well as ADD—described having a job that required her to sit still most of the day as torture. The toll the denial of her need for physical activity took was depression. Others may feed a need to be active by literally eating all of the time, which can then easily create secondary weight or health problems.

Behaviors like fidgeting can be just the tip of the iceberg for people who have not honored their powerful need to be physically active throughout their day. The problem with denying your physical restlessness is that it can lead to depression or feelings of exhaustion. When energy can't find an outlet, it just shuts down—like the crash of a computer—leaving a person feeling empty and depressed. Although an ADD adult with depression usually doesn't feel like doing anything, the cure is sometimes as simple as finding a physical outlet for the suppressed energy. If you struggle with depression or behaviors that involve fidgeting, try to find more ways to express your energy. This could be a simple as planning regular walks around your office or listening to music and letting yourself move to it.

Another way to express your hyperactivity is to be more physically active while doing your regular activities. For example, plan romantic dates to involve hiking rather than long dinners. In my own case, I've structured my private practice so that I rarely schedule clients back to back. This allows me frequent and regular breaks to walk. If I'm doing phone coaching, I also stay active by pacing.

RESTLESSNESS

Whether your hyperactivity causes you to try too hard or has been repressed, it makes waiting almost impossible. Indeed, the most pervasive symptom of ADD is impatience. Impatience can cause you to drive too fast, talk too fast, and interrupt others at every turn. Impatience can make you race past life's most precious moments. Impatience can also drive some to drugs and alcohol, in hopes of slowing down to the pace of others.

One of the most disruptive symptoms of ADD is a time distortion. ADD people are always in high drive, while other people seem to move, talk, and think glacially slowly. This can lead to a constant sense of restlessness in adults with ADD. Moreover, this impatience can quickly turn into hostility if you think people are moving, talking, or thinking slowly just to piss you off.

Stop right now and translate your restlessness into productive energy with five simple steps:

1. Stop, stand still, and consider opening up to a new perspective. Take a few deep breaths and put your attention on the feeling of restlessness.

2. Ask yourself, "Where in my body do I feel this restlessness?"

3. Direct your attention to this physical, bodily sensation of restlessness.

4. Visualize an image that captures the essence of this restlessness.

5. Ask yourself, "How does this image show me the gift in my restlessness?"

Just the process of feeling the sensations on a physical level will give you more control over your activity level. On a deeper level, the visualized image will actually contain some of the energy. And finally, the image you come up with will provide you with a creative reframing for your restlessness. For example, when doing this exercise I once came up with the image of a waterwheel. Because waterwheels are sources of strong, clean energy, this image challenged my idea that I was just spinning my wheels.

The Gift of Restlessness

The ability to contain the feelings of restlessness is a basic life skill for coping with the givens of life; however, there is a much deeper gift in restlessness. In addition to controlling your impatience, you will also want to figure out what guidance may lie in your restlessness. Your restlessness may be a warning that there are better ways to spend your time. Your restlessness may indicate that you are living a false life. Your restlessness may be saying, "Move on!" or "Keep moving!" In order to understand its deeper meaning, you will have to contain and listen to your impatience.

Hagen: Lessons Learned and Stories to Tell

"When Ben Franklin put a key on a kite, he knew something could happen—other people told him, 'You're going to get hit by lightning and die.' People who plan too much are just afraid." When Hagen decided to open his own GNC business—without having had any business experience or classes—people told him he was crazy. Hagen had been working at a GNC store while he studied biology at the University of Central Florida, intending to become a doctor. When he asked his boss for a raise, his boss told him he should open his own store. Six months later, Hagen left school to do just that. "There was no dreaming, no hesitation, no second guessing. I made it happen—and yes, my mom wanted to kill me, but my dad said go for it. Looking back, I wonder why they gave me a franchise—I was clueless! But on the other hand, I was so confident and so sure I would succeed, why wouldn't they? I didn't know I was so clueless, so how could they?"

Hagen and I have had a series of conversations; they started in June of 2007 and continue to this day. I initially contacted him, remembering him as an intelligent and hilarious radio personality who had interviewed me for my first book, *The Gift of ADHD;* he had confided in me then that he, too, had ADD. Like many of the others profiled, Hagen recounted clear, precise visions of a future in which he knew he would succeed. He told me, "I knew I could succeed. I had total confidence." He never thought about what he would do if he failed. And he didn't: his various businesses have been so successful that they have given him complete control over his life.

As a child, Hagen was so wild and hyperactive that his school decided to let him run around freely. This solution was reached after he was held back in third grade. Though Hagen was in a gifted students' program, his hyperactivity was a distraction to others; as a result, his teachers put him into a third- and second-grade combo class. This made the problem even worse, because now he was really bored. His teachers came up with an interesting solution: if

Hagen felt restless and frisky, he should "go to the bathroom and take a little walk."

"A Nonmedicated Pain in the Ass"

Medication was suggested for Hagen, but Hagen's mother refused it. She had seen such drugs turn another child who used to be a terror into a zombie. Hagen's mom told him, "After watching him turn into a zombie, I would never put you on that stuff—I like you more as a nonmedicated pain in the ass." With his teachers' permission to get up and move, Hagen came and went from the classroom as he pleased. He remembers running around on the sidewalk outside of the classroom, then returning to class able to sit still and conform to school norms. Because of this arrangement, he didn't get into trouble.

As Hagen describes it, he was bored because the class moved extremely slowly. When he was bored, he didn't care if he got in trouble because that at least gave him something to do. After his teachers encouraged him to walk off his extra energy, when Hagen got bored he would get up and leave, literally walking out of class. When he returned, the class would have finally moved onto something new. He would take in some more material and then leave again when the pace slowed.

Restlessness Is a Gift

"Restlessness is a gift because it forces me to think." Hagen has a hard time imagining why someone would choose to be "slow and half asleep" rather than "sped up and full of energy" like he is. Hagen is too restless to read a book; he sees this as an advantage. Many people told him it was a bad idea to start a business at the age of twenty-one, without any accounting or business training. He had never even read a book about business and to this day still doesn't read business books. "When you read stuff and it doesn't happen that way in real life, you're in trouble." Hagen believes that business and management cannot be taught. "Even the most perfect business plan never works out. Should you *plan* to have a manager steal from you? Should you *plan* to have a hurricane wipe you out? Just be confident and make decisions until you get it right." Hagen revels in figuring things out on the fly. He believes that overplanning and excessive reading are signs that "thinking has been taken out of society." He sees a great gift in figuring things out on your own.

He scoffs at the engineer who has to read an entire car manual before operating a car. Hagen prefers to just hop in the car and figure it out as he goes along. He doesn't want to approach things with preconceptions—he sees half the fun and challenge of life as figuring things out on his own.

I first met Hagen when he interviewed me for his radio show. I've been a guest now on approximately one hundred radio shows; Hagen is one of the funniest, smartest, and most entertaining hosts I've ever met. Radio show hosts are known for being funny, smart, and entertaining, so the fact that Hagen stands out speaks to his gifts. He told me he would never read a book by a guest before a show. He knew that would make for a dull and boring interview. He didn't even use the media questions from the press kit. He instead let his curiosity and interest drive his explorations of a topic. As the guest being interviewed, it was refreshing not to be asked the same questions from the press kit. Hagen's interest and engagement were evident.

He points to another problem with thinking and planning too much: it can interfere with interpersonal connections. "Running a business is a team; you have to relate to people. You cannot get that from a book." He argues that whether running a business or hosting a radio show, an essential element is the ability to build good relationships. Book learning is not ideal for promoting relationship skills.

Jumping In

Hagen attributes his success to two things: the ability to generate many ideas and the hyperactivity that perpetually drives him to take action rather than just wait for good things to happen.

With the success of his GNC store, Hagen branched out into real estate, tanning salons, and other businesses. When people ask Hagen how he became so successful, he tells them, "I'm not any smarter than anyone else. I'm just not afraid to make decisions and put them into action." While other people delay their dreams in favor of never-ending strategic planning, Hagen takes risks and learns from his mistakes—and he admits he has made mistakes. He describes his present good judgment and maturity as the fruit of bad decisions he made in the past. One such mistake was taking on the management of his stores; this demanded too much of his energy and organization. He realized that his greatest gift is his ability to generate great ideas. He is currently working to turn this ability into a career. "I can sell my ideas to other people and let them manage all the business." Hagen is evolving toward a life that capitalizes on his greatest strengths.

Hagen's hyperactivity provides him with the drive to turn his ideas into reality, whether he is subbing the details out or handling them himself. Because he needs to be in constant motion, he immediately runs with his ideas. Like many ADD adults, Hagen talks about the stress and pressure that get his adrenaline going and allow him to function optimally. As discussed in Captain Ohlrich's profile in chapter 5, adrenaline is an organic neurotransmitter that functions much like the stimulant medication prescribed to ADD adults to help them focus. For Hagen, the risk he takes by immediately jumping into action leads to a surge of adrenaline, which then actually stimulates his capacity to think and generate new ideas. He explains this process with the metaphor of people who have to look over the edge when they are high in a building or overlooking any steep drop. "By looking over the edge, they get scared and have to think what they would do if something happened." The idea is that facing problems head-on forces us to begin problem solving. If we merely avoid risks, we never have to solve the problems those risks entail. By entering into our fear rather than avoiding it, we have no choice but to become creative and think for ourselves.

Planning Is Fear

"To make a decision without much thought of the outcome is critical to accomplishing things." Many would call this recklessness; for Hagen it is a fundamental guiding principle. Four-year-olds, he pointed out, ski down dangerous ski slopes with great agility, almost entirely because of their lack of fear about what could happen to them. These four-year-olds have no skills, no lessons, no books, almost no motor skills, weak muscles, and no expectations about where they are going or even how long the slope is. "They can't even dress themselves in their ski outfits, but they make decisions as the need arises and succeed because they have no fear."

He sees parallels in how he runs his businesses: "My ADD mind constantly generates new ideas, and I have the energy to act on them immediately." He contrasts his strategy for success with that of friends who have been planning for dreams for many years now without making any actual progress. He thinks of a friend who wants to be a designer but whose sewing machine has yet to be used. Hagen believes that planning is fear. For him, success is about being fearless and learning from mistakes. This approach has steered him away from a life of what-ifs and toward a life of fulfillment. Indeed, his hyperactivity propels him to rejigger his life every few years, leading him from one dream to another. For him there are no regrets, "only lessons learned and stories to tell."

CHAPTER 9

Your Emotionally Expressive Gifts

Often, the uncontrolled emotional outbursts of an ADD adult are actually signs of an intense emotional sensitivity. This sensitivity is the ADD quality that can get you into the most trouble. Perhaps you told your supervisor off. Perhaps you fired an employee without realizing the legal tangles it would get you into. Learning to stay connected to your emotional gifts without acting explosively can turn around a life of frequent job changes and failed relationships.

The very same emotional intensity that makes it so easy for you to connect with others can also lead to destructive outbursts when conflicts arise. You may feel that if you don't express your deepest feelings—or even just the ones closest to the surface—then you are not being completely authentic. ADD adults are warriors for authenticity. They demand it from themselves and from others. This is a great gift, but it can also lead to unrealistic expectations, thus creating problems in relationships. While it may be easy for *you* to wear your heart on your sleeve, others may be either disconnected from their feelings or not as willing to express them.

You may feel that others are holding back or being fake when they restrain their emotional connection and expression, whether out of habit or strategy. Because of the great sensitivity and overwhelming impact of your feelings, these emotions come with the sense of self-evident truth. And indeed, they do often reflect reality; however, expressing these emotions may not be in your best interest. If you can catch your emotions in their earliest stage and translate them into information to guide your behavior rather than hijack it, you will then be able to reap the full benefits of this gift.

TRANSLATE IRRITATION INTO INFORMATION

Chances are, your irritation is giving you important information that you need to take action on. However, if you launch into accusations rather than measured inquiries, your effectiveness will be compromised. Instead, every time you feel your irritation begin to rise, ask yourself, "What guidance does this feeling offer me?"

One woman felt that a coworker was encroaching on her territory in a project. Previously she would have launched a verbal attack to protect her space. After we had worked on this issue in therapy, she approached the situation differently. This time, she simply checked with a supervisor to determine if her perceptions were correct. They were. Her irritation was the result of a misunderstanding on the part of the coworker. She took this information and communicated it calmly and collectedly to her coworker, referring her to the supervisor for role clarification. As we processed this incident in therapy, she realized that her irritation had been a valuable guide, giving her accurate information about a coworker's role confusion. It was part of her job to address these issues; treating her irritation as guidance rather than expressing it outright allowed her to do her job that much more competently.

The sticking point for a lot of ADD adults is that they think the fact that they are right justifies any means of addressing the problem. When an ADD adult gets called to the carpet for over-the-top behavior, he is likely to back up his behavior by insisting that he is right. The problem is, he has let emotions rather than the information guide his behavior.

Remember, as right as you may be, it's usually in your best interest to address a problem with a measured course of action. Use the following activity to moderate your response whenever you feel your anger rising. You can also use it with overwhelming sadness or fear.

ACTIVITY: THE THIRTY-SECOND RULE

If a troubling emotion arises, follow the *thirty-second rule:* give yourself permission to feel the emotion, but only for thirty seconds. You may be afraid that if you open to your emotions, you will get lost in them and lose control. This fear may be legitimate—sometimes emotions can disrupt your life. Letting yourself experience emotions in thirty-second chunks is a valuable skill that will allow you to honor your feelings without being dominated by them. One of the main benefits of this practice is that it helps you realize that your emotions don't have to control you—you can control your emotions.

1. When an emotion dominates your attention, set aside thirty seconds to go deeper into it. Breathe into the feeling. See if you can imagine your breath touching the feeling. As you breathe into the feeling, imagine it becoming more intense. Remember, you are only going to do this for thirty seconds, so don't be afraid of going deeper. Imagine turning up the volume on the emotion; imagine it becoming more and more intense. Feelings are like a waves: they get more intense, they crest, and then they get smaller and go away. With only ten seconds left, imagine your feeling slipping away, just like the wave after it crests.

Breathe deeply and let the feeling go. Many people are surprised to find that, by using this image of a wave, they can let go of a feeling fairly easily.

2. Try to translate the emotion into a form of guidance. For example, if you are angry, you may need to communicate your boundaries or needs more clearly. If you are sad, you may need to find support for your grief. If you are afraid, you may need to determine if what you are afraid of is a likely or unlikely possibility. If it is an unlikely possibility, try to refocus your energy. If it is a likely possibility, begin to seek resources for addressing it.

3. If you find yourself stuck in an emotion, continue to process it either by talking it through with another person or journaling about it. If the emotion reflects difficult life events or tragic losses, spend ten minutes writing about the events and fifteen minutes writing about the remarkable gifts you must have to have survived them.

The Thirty-Second Rule on the Fly

Here are three steps you can use any time: (1) breathe into the emotion, (2) stay with it for thirty seconds, and (3) find the emotion in your body. Finding the emotion in your body will help you get more of a handle on it, giving you more control. Taking just these three steps can give you control of the emotion. As a result, you will be much less likely to follow an impulse you will later regret.

THE LIMITS OF AUTHENTICITY

During one of my classes, a student in the front row rolled her eyes every time I mentioned a requirement of the course. When I highlighted the importance of being able to articulate both sides of an argument—even if it was a position a student didn't personally agree with—she let out a huge, exasperated sigh. Needless to say, I invited her to speak with me after class. When asked to explain her disruptive behavior, she told me that she was "just being authentic," that she had learned in her other classes that being authentic was the most important thing a therapist could do.

Her predicament was similar to that which ADD adults face every day. Authenticity *is* the most important quality that a therapist can bring to psychotherapy. However, it is not the *only* quality—and, when taken to extremes, it can clearly be disruptive or, even worse, destructive. Like many ADD adults, I hold authenticity as one of my highest personal values. But to achieve core desires, authenticity is best paired with other qualities. One way to achieve a healthy balance between authenticity and other qualities is to practice the power of flexible thinking. The following activity will help you with this.

ACTIVITY: THE POWER OF "AND"

If you don't practice flexible thinking, you may find that expressing your short-term authenticity interferes with the expression of your long-term authenticity. For example, if you can't make a living because you keep losing jobs over your emotional expressiveness, you won't be able to honor a core desire to translate your emotional expressiveness to bring about healing or creativity. If you desperately want to be in a relationship but are so sensitive to rejection that you take no risks, you are not serving your deepest authenticity.

1. Circle all of the following statements that resonate with you:

- I am loving being authentic and maintaining mutually satisfying relationships.

- I am loving being authentic and using my authenticity to heal relationships in my workplace.

- I am loving being authentic and keeping professional boundaries.

• I am loving being authentic and using my authenticity as a force for creativity and success.

• I am loving being authentic and creating sweet and nourishing relationships.

• I am loving being authentic and increasing my connection with others.

• I am loving being authentic and increasing my power.

• I am loving being authentic and using my authenticity to create abundance with ease.

• I am loving being authentic and gaining the loyalty of employees.

2. Review the statements that resonate the most with you. If you were to channel the power of flexible thinking, how would you use your emotional sensitivity to fulfill the goals that most of us hope to achieve—more healing, more intimacy, and more power in professional settings? Write about this question in your journal.

3. Commit to one small action that will require you to be authentic in a way that will also honor your deeper core demands. For example, you might

practice translating your anger at a romantic partner into a list of needs you'd like to have met. In this way, you honor your authenticity while exercising skill and care in how you express it.

Focusing Feels Like Cutting Myself Off

Many ADD adults report that when they focus, it actually feels like they're cutting a part of themselves off—their emotional sensitivity. In speaking of ADHD, psychologist James Hillman writes, "Children so categorized, and adults too, are often those with above-average intelligence, given to daydreams, and with such widely open sensitive souls that their 'ego' behavior is noncompliant and disorganized" (1996, 126). Mike, a student of mine with ADD, spoke to me about what it feels like for such a widely open, sensitive soul to focus and narrow his range of awareness by following rules or paying attention to details. The following excerpts are taken from a series we taped and transcribed for a research project in 1998.

> *The whole idea of having to focus, I don't like, I don't like at all ... For me it takes such an effort to focus because I have to cut off so many things ... There's a long process of dulling certain senses and feelings and emotions—and because it's so long there are a number of things I'm nullifying and blinding myself to ... It could be any number*

of thoughts or exterior stimuli. I don't like to do that.

When I'm enjoying life, experiencing all it has to offer, I don't want to sit down and read a book. I feel as though I'm doing myself an injustice by paying attention to one single entity when I perceive so many other things. It's so hard. It's such a challenge to stay focused when you're conscious of other things. I'll be reading a book and something else will come up, and I won't know where it's come from, but I'll have to push it back down, sweep it under the rug. And then, as I continue reading, something else will come up. They're like impulses and I can't control them. Before I never had to, I never wanted to—to me that was just what life was. Impulses are [alive] to me, so having to quell those I don't like ... There's a feeling of discomfort...

[Impulses are] what make life interesting—not knowing what's going to happen in the next instant, living life like it's one big giant impulse, like it's just a feeling, nothing more than that. Sometimes it's fun to not even inhibit yourself and just go with things and see where they take you. It's brilliant to me to go to unprecedented, unknown realms ... I feel like I'm taking off, going somewhere, I don't know where, and then all of the sudden I figure it out, and it's like bam!

> *[When I'm focusing] I'm kind of steering myself away from that, away from a whole boundaryless universe out there.*

For Mike, having to focus on a single task is to be cut off from his emotional sensitivity. To pay attention he must deaden and numb his vibrant inner world, he must shove his emotions under a rug. For Mike, the process of narrow focus causes an uncomfortable loss of an expansive state of consciousness. When Mike focuses, he loses both his emotional world and the way it connects him to the "whole boundaryless universe out there."

UNLEASHING YOUR INNER LANDSCAPE

Because, as an ADD adult, emotional sensitivity comes easily to you, you may not fully value the great gift it has to offer. Our own gifts are often hard for us to see because we tend to believe that what is easy cannot be valuable. We equate hard work and struggle with contribution. However, our greatest contribution may come precisely from those abilities that come to us as easily as falling off a log. The things we do best often feel the easiest to us.

When you value what you can contribute through your emotional sensitivity, you will begin to nourish and nurture your natural ability. For example, emotional sensitivity often cries out for creative expression. By expressing your experiences creatively, you can offer healing to others, revealing to them deep layers of their inner landscape that they do not have ready access to. One psychologist writes that "Charles Darwin tells us that it is precisely the function of art to 'sap the moralistic timidity' that prevents us from examining feeling states and attitudes that were previously regarded as off-bounds ... [Artists] can be seen as venturing into psychological experiences at the very border of human comprehension, and attempting, through artistic expression, to bring order to them, to communicate them, and perhaps to hear some response to their message" (Hazell 2003, 94). Think of the contributions of Vincent van Gogh, whose visual sensitivity made the world come alive in new ways for the rest of us; or of Jim Morrison, whose musical sensitivity moved a generation; or writers and philosophers like Shakespeare, Tolstoy, and Kierkegaard, who reveal our own selves to us.

When you are emotionally sensitive, you find it difficult to repress or suppress your inner responses to the world. The more sensitive you are, the more you crave to channel your experiences into some form of creative expression. Indeed, emotional sensitivity may be the root cause of creativity. In studying creative genius, English professor John Briggs discovered that "it is good to tune into feelings before they get abstracted into a thought. People who can do this are able to directly tune into data of far greater complexity. Such sensitivity fosters creativity and the ability to see things in new ways" (2000, 56).

It is important to honor your impulse to translate your sensitivity into creativity. Don't limit yourself by thinking that creative expression has to be skillful or lucrative. Finding and embracing a creative outlet is much like taking a dog cooped up in a small apartment out to a vast natural landscape and unleashing her.

Your creativity will not only enrich your life and that of others, it will also be powerfully healing for you. Many psychological symptoms can be traced to a dammed-up creative expression. When you don't bring forth the art that is within you, the creative force can turn ugly. Addictions can sometimes be attempts to repress emotional sensitivity; the very act of unleashing this sensitivity can mitigate the need for the dulling effects of drugs, alcohol, shopping, sex, pornography, compulsive busyness, and so on.

HOW TO AVOID AN ENTIRELY FALSE LIFE

Using your emotional sensitivity to create—whether that creation is a painting, a song, a short story, or something else—can enable you to get a handle on it. And by expressing your inner world, you can liberate others. The more of our natural instincts we suppress, the more our lives become meaningless. Your expressiveness can give others the permission they need to begin to recognize their own shut-down inner worlds. In *The Death of Ivan Ilyich,* Leo Tolstoy wrote about how the suppression of emotional sensitivity can cause us to waste our lives:

> It occurred to him that his scarcely perceptible attempts to struggle against what was considered good by the most highly placed people, those scarcely noticeable impulses which he had immediately suppressed, might have been the real thing, and all the rest false. And his professional duties and the whole arrangement of his life and of his family, and all his social and official interests, might all have been false. (As quoted in Harris 2007, 108)

ADD adults typically avoid this tragedy. Because of your emotional sensitivity and impulsiveness, you often cannot cut off even "scarcely noticeable impulses" in the service of conformity as others do. This may be the most formidable gift of ADD adults. You may fail miserably in following directions, in paying close attention to details, and finding any semblance of organization, but you are often irresistibly drawn to spend your time doing what enlivens you, even to your own exasperation. Although you may chide yourself for your inability to get with the program or be in sync with others, you may actually be saving yourself from a greater tragedy: an entirely false life.

Your emotional sensitivity allows you to get your own needs met. The emblem of emotional sensitivity gone bad is the temper tantrum. If tantrums didn't cause so many problems, they would actually be a highly effective way of getting needs met—with a tantrum, no one is ever left wondering, "Now what does she *really* want here?" The challenge for you is to communicate your needs tastefully rather than through tantrums.

Your needs are signposts to your destiny; your ability to have a tantrum may be important for keeping you on the path of this destiny. (Now you only need to learn to get what you want without losing face in the process!) Needs are also the basic fuel that keeps us moving through life. Research reveals that even just getting in touch with a need can alleviate depression, even when that need isn't met (Rice and Greenberg 1984). In my practice, I have observed that just helping clients identify their needs often leads to their figuring out how to meet these needs. For example, a person who is lonely will be propelled to make social connections once he feels the fullness of his need for relationships. Indeed, needs may be necessary to keep us passionately engaged in life. When I work with suicidal individuals, the first question I ask is "What do you need and how can I help you meet that need?" Often suicidal individuals have a hard time even identifying their needs.

If you don't identify your needs, you can't consciously work toward meeting them. Indeed, to truly meet a need, you must first know that it exists. Then, the more intense the need, the more motivated you will be to figure out how to meet it. This is good news for ADD adults, who often find that their needs have an intrusive quality. Adults without this level of sensitivity can easily plow through life attending to other people's needs and living up to others' expectations, but never making their own needs a priority.

At some point in your life, you've probably beaten yourself up over one of the signal symptoms of ADD: not doing what you are told. This is often the chief complaint of parents and teachers seeking a diagnosis of ADD for a child. But not doing what you are told is really just an insistence on living your life in alignment with your own agenda rather than someone else's.

The wisdom literature of the ages tells us that knowing who we are is the most important pursuit we have as humans. Becoming who we are meant to be demands an avid interest in tracking our own needs. While ADD adults may be chided for focusing too much on their own agenda, ignoring your agenda can also take an enormous toll. Ignoring your agenda can lead to a life of "quiet desperation"—or, more often, a life of such loud desperation that a cocktail of prescription medications or a raging addiction is required to soothe it.

Take Your Troubles, Leave Your Symptoms

It may help you to remember the difference between trouble and symptoms. Trouble is what you get when others are upset by your devotion to your own agenda. Symptoms are what you get when you ignore your agenda. For example, if you choose to honor your need for adventure in a way that other people don't understand, you will get trouble. However, if you try to fit your need for experience into a smaller life, you will get symptoms of depression, anxiety, and despair. If, at the top of your game, you tell people it's time for you to make a change, you will get trouble. On the other hand, if you stay, you will get symptoms of porn addiction, gambling addiction, or other compulsions. The sad truth is that often when we make decisions to avoid trouble, we create symptoms.

One of the enormous gifts of being an ADD adult is that you are more likely to choose trouble over symptoms. However, you may beat yourself up for your tendency to get in trouble. Begin to free yourself from this cycle of self-recrimination by translating your guilt into a sign of progress.

If honoring your own agenda means breaking free from commitments that are helpful to others but a drain on you, you will get trouble and guilt. For example, one woman decided that her agenda required her to travel for pleasure. She wasn't sure she could explain to her family that her travel plans didn't include visiting them. She felt enormous guilt over her decision, but also a sense that it was urgent for her to start trusting her own agenda, even when it was hard to explain to others. In our work together, we reviewed how a lifetime of choices made to fulfill the expectations of others had depleted her. I helped her to translate her guilt into a sign of pursuing personal fulfillment. Every time she felt guilty and began to think about how others might be mad at her, she was to visualize a champagne glass being filled with champagne. This image reminded her of the joy of celebrating her own agenda, of being filled rather than depleted.

Choose Your Agenda Over Your Addiction

The good thing about intense emotional sensitivity is that it trumps the rational mind. This means that you may often feel it's urgent to do something without a clear explanation for why. This inner sense of needing to do something—or your agenda—is often about being plugged in to something bigger than you are. As a result, it can be difficult to explain to others why you must do what you need to do. (You don't usually need to explain it to yourself because its importance is typically self-evident.)

Much of my work with ADD adults is about helping them trust their own agenda. I am often amazed by how much more wisdom a person's agenda will have than her rational planning mind. For example, one mother realized her agenda involved getting assistance with her children rather than always personally catering to them. She found a mother's helper and accepted help from her own family. When she trusted her agenda, she found herself creating a successful business that gave her family a lifestyle free from financial struggles and arguments. Her marriage improved, and she found she enjoyed parenting more because she was now more emotionally available to connect with her children and felt less tension. When she had ignored her agenda, instead catering to her children, she had cycled downward into depression. When she honored her agenda, her children had less contact with her but they had a happy, vibrant mother, and the financially stressed home filled with marital tensions now became a much more carefree place. Thus, honoring her own agenda proved to be healing not only for her, but for her family, too.

The good thing about your emotional sensitivity is that it makes your agenda almost impossible to ignore. Even your emotional outbursts can be fierce protectors in the service of your agenda. Those who are more controlled can unintentionally manage away their own agenda. I've been amazed by how any individual's agenda—irrespective of whether the individual has ADD—will seek expression even when the individual himself has chosen not to follow it. If you trust your agenda, life will usually go much easier than if you ignore it. If you don't leave a job that is harming you, events will often conspire to force you out of it. If you don't honor your need for rest and rejuvenation, events will often conspire to give you time off.

Don't confuse your agenda with getting your way in a petty power struggle. Your agenda involves connecting with people and callings that will meet your deepest needs. Power struggles can happen when you become polarized against someone whom you perceive is trying to control you for the sake of asserting power. Your emotional sensitivity may cause you to lose control in such a power struggle. If you want to know how to handle a power struggle, refer back to your agenda. If your agenda is to create a nurturing family environment and you are fighting with your spouse about unnecessary spending, recognize that you are engaged in a power struggle and soothe your emotional bristling. On the other hand, if you are fighting with your spouse about the need to make time for family recreation, honor your agenda and your emotions, but remember that explosive outbursts may work against your agenda to create a healthy, nourishing family life.

Your defiance and emotional outbursts usually reflect your devotion to your agenda. The problem is that when others block your agenda in the service of their own expectations or control issues, defiance and hostility may become a bad habit.

FIGHT THE GOOD FIGHT

It is good to be inelastic but tactful in pressing forward with your agenda, whether it be taking over a company or freeing up time for recreation in your family life. To gain *relationship capital,* or the goodwill of others who can help you achieve your agenda, handle conflicts not directly related to your agenda with grace.

ACTIVITY: TRANSLATE INSULTS INTO INSIGHTS

Because of your intense sensitivity, even constructive criticism from others can cut like an insult. You may also have to deal with actual, mean-spirited insults. You can gain from insults and criticism by mining them for valuable insights, either into how you are perceived by others or how you really are.

1. Write down a recent criticism or insult that hurt your feelings. For example, maybe an employee told you that you were unreasonable and were treating her like a child.

2. Search your memory of the events surrounding the insult or criticism for any insight that might lead you to understanding yourself better. For example, maybe you'll realize that the reason you were treating your employee like a child is because you feel superior to her. Once you recognize this feeling of superiority, you can learn to see how it might serve you and how you might handle it more skillfully. (Many ADD adults feel that their ability to think and act more quickly than others makes them superior, but wouldn't dare express this even to themselves. The key is to embrace and channel this feeling of superiority in a way that will further your agenda rather than cause it to stall out.)

Dr. Stephanie Moulton Sarkis: The Power of Passion

"It's good to express emotions, to lay it all out on table: this is how I'm feeling, this is it. I don't repress it," Stephanie Moulton Sarkis told me over the phone.

"I get the help I need; no one has to do guesswork." Stephanie has channeled her ADD into a successful career as a psychologist, coach, and author. I interviewed her over the phone and in a series of e-mails in the summer of 2007.

Stephanie is the author of *10 Simple Solutions to Adult ADD: How to Overcome Chronic Distraction and Accomplish Your Goals* (2006) and *Making the Grade with ADD: A Student's Guide to Succeeding in College with Attention Deficit Disorder* (2008). For Stephanie, emotional sensitivity means passion. She channels this passion into writing, a lifelong interest and her signature strength.

Stephanie believes that, as an ADD adult, finding your signature strength is key to your success. Embracing your signature strength will not only help you find personal fulfillment, it will also provide an outlet for your passionate intensity. She tells her many ADD clients that by channeling their passion, they can change the world.

While there is much debate in the field on whether medications inhibit or facilitate creativity, Stephanie finds that medication is necessary for her to reach her full potential. Because Adderall allows her to focus more on her writing, it gives her a great outlet for her energy and passion. "I can sit now, and write an entire chapter in one sitting." In addition, the medication also helps both her driving and her ability to focus on conversations; she often recommends that clients consider medication in their treatment approach.

Although Stephanie knew she had ADD for most of her life, she wasn't formally diagnosed until she was twenty-three, when she found that the demands of graduate school brought her ADD traits to the forefront and sought treatment. During our interview, Stephanie spontaneously connected her emotional sensitivity to each of the other four gifts I have outlined: intuition, creativity, exuberance, and ecological consciousness.

Interpersonal Intuition

Stephanie believes that her success as a psychotherapist is not just in spite of, but because of her ADD. She directly connects her emotional sensitivity to her empathy or interpersonal intuition. "My ADD is a key part of being a therapist. I'm empathic; I get where kids are coming from. I'm a good judge of character and can tell what someone's like."

When Stephanie works with families, she can hear what everyone is saying, even when everyone is talking at the same time. This is facilitated by a key strength of ADD adults—the ability to take in information on multiple channels at the same time. She can also change tracks quickly, which helps her to follow non sequiturs. Like many of the other successful ADD adults profiled in this book, Stephanie uses her ability to tune in to other people's needs in her work. Because she understands what others need, she can nurture them.

Creativity

Stephanie also connects her emotional sensitivity to her creativity. Her writing and her creativity feed each other, the writing providing a container for her emotional sensitivity. Although Stephanie is very creative and can generate a lot of ideas, she needs someone without ADD to help her follow through.

ADD adults have a tendency to *hyperfocus,* or to become deeply engaged for long periods of time in material they are passionate about, typically with heightened attention. Stephanie explains this tendency as a form of creative absorption. For example, when she listens to music she has enough perspective to be aware of things like pitch and tone. However, when she plays music she begins to hyperfocus. Because she's not aware of anything else going on around her, she can be completely in tune with the music, amplifying her creative expression. "I love to play the music, to feel the music," said Stephanie, "it's a whole experience."

Exuberance

Stephanie also makes a strong link between her emotional sensitivity and her exuberance or hyperactivity. Her interests are broad, and because of her high levels of excitement, she always has, as she put it, "an iron in the fire." She loves to travel, cook, write, play music, and be involved in community service. When she spoke to me about her travel plans—a catalogue of personal desires, many of which have already become realities—I could hear the telltale ADD exuberance in her voice. She has traveled in North America, Europe, and China.

Ecological Consciousness

Stephanie also spoke about another gift of ADD: a connection to nature. She told me her emotional sensitivity compels her to take action; she feels connected to her community, the universe, and other living things. She is directly involved in advocacy for homeless pets and has two dogs who were rescued from the streets. "Because I feel a connection with other living things, I'm sensitive to the suffering of animals. We have an obligation to speak for living things that can't speak for themselves."

How She Manages Sensitivity

As a psychotherapist and author, Stephanie has thought deeply about how to channel ADHD characteristics into gifts. When we spoke, she highlighted the importance of self-care. "You have to choose self-care over codependency." The ability to tune in to others' needs with uncanny accuracy can easily be transformed into a codependent striving to meet these same needs. Because she tends to be immersed in others' emotions, Stephanie told me she has to be vigilant about what she is feeling. "Your heart engages before your brain does to make the connection a little smoother. I have to slow down, say, 'Wait a minute, what am I feeling here?'"

Some of the practices she uses to help her stay balanced in her own core include deep breathing, eating well, exercising regularly, and getting out in nature every day. She believes, as do many ADD experts, that exercise and being in nature can change how her brain functions.

She summarized the gifts of ADD—her own and those she has observed in her clients—as "what you see is what you get; not a lot of pretenses, so our relationships are more genuine. We ADD people are very charismatic, never boring; we have a real joie de vivre." While almost all experts have noted the association of charisma with ADD, for Stephanie it is front and center—she attributes much of her success directly to this and other qualities of ADD.

CHAPTER 10

Promise and Pitfalls

As you have read through this book, you have likely been aware that the many gifts discussed interact complexly with ADD's obvious pitfalls. For every wildly successful ADD businessperson, there is one who lands in prison for tax evasion—whether due to disregard for details or pure recklessness. For every ADD adult sailing through life on her charisma, there is one caught in a downward spiral of sensation seeking, one impulse feeding on another. For every great leader, there is a gang member using his leadership gifts to enlist others in a life of crime.

Even in those who function at high levels, the tension between the promise and pitfalls of ADD is evident. You may have lost relationships because you couldn't organize yourself and others tired of acting as your personal assistant. Your drive and energy may have brought you great success but made it almost impossible to slow down and savor a single moment. The gifts ADD confers do not eliminate the many challenges and failures that will be faced by an individual in a culture that does not value differences. Even with success, you may always feel like the proverbial round peg in a square hole.

THE PROMISE AND PITFALLS OF THE DIAGNOSIS

The promise of getting a diagnosis is that suddenly what may have seemed like a personal failing has a name. The pitfall of getting a diagnosis is that while ADD may roll off the tongue these days like a hip new fad, it is classified as a mental disorder. The label illuminates at the very same time that it incapacitates. And the label can easily become a permission slip for problem behavior; for example, for kids to stop working or for husbands to cheat on their wives because "my ADD made me do it."

Impact of the Diagnosis

"The idea that I'm not talented makes me sick." For my student Mike, the label of ADD itself made him feel sick. It increased his sense that he was indeed different, but in a way that was abnormal or "sick." His response illustrates author Michael Ventura's contention that "diagnoses act like computer viruses, changing and erasing memories" (Hillman and Ventura 1992, 74). Similarly, Hillman has warned, "The force of diagnostic stories cannot be exaggerated. Once one has been written into a particular clinical fantasy with its expectations, its typicalities, its character traits, and the rich vocabulary it offers for recognizing oneself, one then begins to recapitulate one's life into the shape of the story" (Hillman 1983, 15),

Mike's diagnosis contributed to his sense of worthlessness, which then exacerbated or created the very symptoms to confirm the negative aspects of the label. When I observed Mike beat himself up about his C grades in my course, I asked him why he didn't ask for accommodations for his ADD. What follows is his response.

> *Probably because I don't like to say, "I have a disorder" ... It's not fun to say "I have a disorder"—does that mean I can't succeed? Am I already getting off on the wrong foot? It's really defeating to think that I don't have what everybody else has. I still have the perception that I am someone talented ...* This idea that I'm not talented makes me sick.
>
> *I do think that I'm on par with other students here ... [But] I do believe there's something different about me. I don't know what it is. That's the only value I put on that label—I'm different so I'm labeled with something. I really fight the idea that it's a disorder; it really has such a devastating impact. I use the words "hazed," "being somewhat confused," "in a shroud of doubt." When you're struggling for confidence, something so trivial as an ADHD label [can be a problem]. I shouldn't allow it to pervade life, but yet, repeated experiences of failure in different arenas seem to confirm it.*

> *Somewhere deep down there's still a tiny morsel of belief that I'm someone equal, I'm just as good as everyone else. It's so hard to deal with when someone says, "You're just not quite there." Basically what that says is "You're wrong and there's a flaw somewhere and you need to be more realistic, you need to accept this disorder because you're not quite there." It goes a lot farther than saying I have a problem reading books...*
>
> *Somewhere deep down I feel I have potential, but when this thing says I'm behind, it basically says ... [I] don't even know [myself] ... I don't think success is out of my reach—or prosperity and happiness and all those great things—but ADHD says it's going to be a lot more difficult for [me]. [It says,] "There's something wrong with you; you're wrong in thinking that there's an equality ... You're somewhat behind; you're underdeveloped, retarded in some aspects." Coupled with the experiences I've had, it's almost a survival instinct now to avoid things that could put [me] in a harmful environment.*

Mike's response suggests that his avoidance of academic pursuits is, at least in part, a result of the diagnosis. Having been told that he has a "deficit disorder," he avoids the arena (academic) in which he understands himself to be flawed. His lack of interest and motivation in this arena can be attributed to what he calls a "survival instinct." Typically, this kind of lack of interest is taken to be a symptom of the disorder; Mike's experience, however, suggests that this behavior may actually be a symptom of the diagnosis. His experience also poignantly illustrates the extent to which a label can impact your core sense of self.

I once told a journalist that I didn't understand why everyone was so worried about pro athletes taking steroids when no one was making much of a fuss about the fact that four million children take stimulants to do better in school. She said that steroids aren't used to treat a mental disorder. For me this is where the rubber hits the road. An ADD diagnosis is made on performance deficits; thus, the main impulse to medicate ADD is directly related to performance demands. Similarly, the impetus for using steroids is to meet or exceed performance demands. I believe that ADD is a difference that leads to performance deficits mainly in settings that emphasize fact-finding over creativity, innovation, or leadership. Unfortunately, the primary demands of most educational and work settings are to follow directions and pay attention to details.

THE PROMISE

The promise for the ADD adult is that these narrow demands are changing. Below is an e-mail I received from Steve Prevett (profiled in chapter 4) that articulates the irony, heartbreak, and tragedy of viewing ADD as a mental disorder. While offering a personal observation, his comments also reflect ideas of some of today's leading thinkers on what our culture is evolving toward (for example, Thomas Friedman 2006a; Daniel Pink 2005; and Christine Comaford-Lynch 2007).

> *Most global corporations now spend enormous energy (and money) in retraining people to think "outside the box," create new ideas, break away from old regimes or paradigms, and envision new ways of doing business. Markets move so fast now, competition is so fierce and global, that if large companies don't have this "agility" to respond to rapidly changing consumer demands then they know they will fail. That's why my global engineering company allowed (and then positively encouraged) me to start the new "virtual" business rather than just take over an existing "old style" business unit. They encouraged me to break rules, set new standards, and, well, go a bit crazy. Perfect for me!*

So why do schools focus so much on rules, systems, and structure? [On] turning out kids who do what they're told, when they're told—and probably how they're told? I guess that's okay if you're feeding students into places where this is needed, like the army, but as well as being hugely uncomfortable (to put it mildly) for kids with ADD/ADHD, this just doesn't fit the needs of modern business.

This disconnect between the education system and business is bigger than ever ... It's the kids with ADD who can lead the way here. If they were encouraged and nurtured to explore and expand their ADD traits like creativity, impulsiveness, and drive rather than "fit in" with an out-of-date curriculum, then companies that thrive on innovation would be queuing up to employ them...

Interestingly, it's American companies that lead the way in embracing this out-of-box creativity ... I always remember a story told to me by an associate in a major U.S. computing company about why they didn't care what people looked like or wore to the office. Apparently they had a guy who used to sit on a piece of synthetic grass in the corner of the office and looked a bit like a hippie—but it was okay, because he was one

> *of the guys who invented a core Internet technology, so they allowed his unusual ways!*

The promise for ADD adults is that the world is changing in ways that will not only accommodate these differences but will actually create a high demand for them. If you can learn some basic skills for focusing your energy, paying attention to details, and listening to others, you can go far. The promise inherent in ADD will be amplified to the extent that you can name and therefore look for its gifts.

Below, I will share my own story of finding my way toward standing up for my gifts rather than patching up weaknesses.

My Story: Promise and Pitfalls

Having my life flooded with ADD adults since writing *The Gift of ADHD* (2005) has felt like a homecoming to me. I have nearly every symptom of ADD in spades. For me, ADD is a motor that drives me and doesn't let me rest.

I'm a Bozo on the Bus, Too

For a long time, I really believed that other people were moving in slow motion just to piss me off. One day it came as a revelation that other people really were just moving at a rate that was comfortable for them. The difficulty with the listening that gets ADD adults in trouble all the time is related to this feeling of being speeded up. It's hard to listen to others when it feels as if they are thinking and talking in slow motion. This quality is the one that causes me the most emotional pain, the feeling of being lonely, like being a lone speed-freak driver in the carpool lane while others drive in synchrony at a safe and stable speed.

For me, ADD is about evaporating into the people, the places, the music, and the rhythm of where I am. I can't hear what you're saying because my attention has dissolved, carried on the waves of absorption in feelings, reactions, opinions, loves, delights, frustrations, irritations—all links forging my relationship with others. It is exactly this quality of attention connected to the hearts and minds of others that makes it exceedingly difficult to follow directions, listen closely, and focus on details.

I have argued that this inability to pay attention and stay focused is driven by an underlying gift of relational intelligence. It's hard to pay attention when you are intensely attuned to relationships, aware of emotional undercurrents and breaches of connection. Attention is derailed by emotional attunement to others.

Interestingly, the same quality that gets me into trouble in my social relationships disappears entirely and even reverses itself in my work as a psychotherapist. The relational intelligence that can make it difficult for me to pay attention in classrooms, conversations, meetings, or any other dull proceeding turned out to be central to the task of being a therapist and therefore a great gift. Therapy is essentially the establishment of a relationship. You monitor and repair this ongoing alliance in the service of supporting another person in healing her life. I think certain careers are a great match for the ADD mind, and being a psychotherapist is one of those.

ADD in the Consulting Room

In *The Gift of ADHD* I wrote that spaciness can actually be seen as a gift of reading other people's unconscious. By *unconscious,* I simply mean any feelings, thoughts, or intentions that people don't directly acknowledge or admit, sometimes even to themselves. Sigmund Freud (1963) wrote that the best approach for a therapist to contact the unconscious is to adopt a stance of free-floating attention. I argue that this stance is precisely how an ADD person operates on a daily basis. While in my daily life the hyperactivity dominates, when I work with a client I slow down and allow the free-floating attention to dominate. Tapping into this quality purposely, I invite clients to slow down to catch up with their own unconscious.

When I work with ADD clients, their expert ability to detect BS sometimes makes it feel as if the tables have turned on me. It's common for an ADD client's ferocious relational attunement to call me on any inauthenticity, any overreliance on procedural elements of therapy as a barrier to closeness. An ADD client reads me like a book and routs out any note of falseness. The ADD client's ability to see barriers to relationship, to sensitively monitor any moment when I'm not walking my talk, is a great gift because most often they are right on. The challenge for me as a therapist is to show a client how his precise and accurate BS detector can cause him to become unreachable.

Devalued Gifts

The relational intelligence of ADD leads to self-doubt because it will almost always be invalidated. Anyone who calls a person on her BS will predictably be given the feedback that he is wrong. Few people will admit that the irreverent, read-others-like-a-book quality is right on the mark. There is a reason the other person may not be expressing clearly her emotional state, and those same reasons often lead her to tell the ADD person that his perceptions are wrong. So an ADD person goes through the world saying that the emperor is not wearing any clothes and constantly being told that the emperor is indeed wearing clothes. As a result of this devaluation of the perceptions that are at the heart of his gift, the person's self-esteem may suffer.

What Not to Do in Therapy

My struggles with ADD brought me to therapy, which mysteriously became a stepping-stone not only to healing but to a lifelong purpose and career choice. It also fueled my determination to reverse the sickening trend toward focusing on what's wrong while virtually ignoring what's right. In therapy, discussions focused on how my passionate engagement in my career was compulsive workaholism, my resentment of abuses of power was oppositional defiance, and my carefree spirit was a kind of acting out. It was only through intuition and friendships and alliances outside of the mental health field that I learned that I was an intense and wacky chick with brass cojones who had found my sweet spot.

The failure of therapy to reflect this light back to me showed me what *not* to do as a therapist and taught me that if I'm going to hold a mirror up to another person, it should be a shining one showing gifts, strengths, and valiant effort in the face of darkness. The carnival mirror of the mental health system, with its insults and injuries, has done enough damage.

I share all this to meet head-on the criticism that presenting ADD as a gift is a Pollyannaish fantasy. The way out of despair and punishing shame is to find the things you do well and focus on those. By following this approach of doing what I love, focusing on what I do well, I was able to turn this deficit disorder into a series of advanced degrees, books, workshops, a totally self-determined career, and a happy family life. Looking for the gifts in ADD has given me this ability to transmute impulsivity, hyperactivity, and distractibility into creativity, exuberance, intuition, sensitivity, and attunement to nature. I've made this mental shift to focus on strengths, and you can do the same. By planning a life that builds on your strengths rather than patching up your weaknesses, you can find that place where your greatest gifts find expression in meeting the needs of the world.

Vishnu, one of my clients, offered to share how this reframing led to healing for him. While the other profiles in this book are all of ADD people who were successful *before* having bumped into the strategies presented in this book, Vishnu's story illustrates the quantum leap you can take just by switching from patching up weaknesses to embracing your strengths. I spoke with Vishnu weekly in my office and occasionally by phone for five months; our consultation is ongoing.

Vishnu: From Troubled Founder to Poet CEO

Vishnu came to see me at a critical juncture in his life. An intriguing opportunity had just opened up for him: he had the chance to move from creative genius to a powerful, controlling force. But he questioned this move as possibly leading him toward "selling his soul."

When I first met Vishnu, I was immediately impressed by his gifts. I felt left in the dust by Vishnu's intelligence, insight, and ability to make rapid-fire connections. Vishnu is a contemporary Renaissance man or Enlightenment intellectual—someone with a wide-ranging intellect, reminiscent of da Vinci, Michelangelo, and Benjamin Franklin. Our sessions were filled with recitations of poetry (his own and that of the greats), references to quantum physics, and explorations of everything from the ultimate questions to karma, from metaphysics to Buddhist practices. But like the Enlightenment intellectuals who mixed the arts with revolutionary plans, Vishnu also used me as his sounding board for strategizing high-stake negotiations. (Vishnu is both a technology executive and the creator of various technological innovations.)

I marveled at the seamless transitions between his accounts of power plays and creative pursuits. When he told me about his involvement in writing and film directing, without missing a beat I reflected back to him the Woody Allen/Augusten Burroughs comedic writing genius I easily imagined him to be, after having had sessions devolve into laughter even in the face of his life's darker events. His many roles included leader, technology innovator, writer, film director, and revolutionary; his flurry of gifts was dizzying. Once, when working through some key negotiations with him, I watched him transform from a debater making a case to a visionary leader. All of the sudden he tapped into his ability to see a future and made himself—and the vision he saw—irresistibly compelling. I said, "That's it, that's your power as a leader—to unleash devotion to your agenda by creating this vision." "Yes, I'm an evangelist, too," he replied, seeing exactly the subtle shift I had felt.

Time to Take the Steering Wheel

I saw immediately that Vishnu's problem was going to be integrating and finding a container for his whopping talent. Not only was he a creative prodigy, he was co-opting the skills of industry heavy hitters around him like a gathering storm. Combining the creativity of ADD with the desire to create his own rules, he was a force to be reckoned with. His identity had calcified around his reputation as a creative wizard, and he struggled with the question of whether he could broaden this identity to encompass this ability to lead. He didn't want to betray the poet in him.

Vishnu's nightly dreams reflected his fear of taking over the steering wheel—literally. He dreamed of sitting in the back of a car while it drove off a cliff. We worked through his dream together using methods adapted from David Jenkins's *Dream RePlay* (2005). I invited him to imagine it again, this time saying,

"Pull the car over; I'm driving," before the car careened over the cliff. He replayed the dream in his imagination, but this time he took control, driving the car, preventing it from hurling off of the cliff. Within days he reported dramatic changes in his life. He shifted gears, making choices based on what he wanted and who he wanted to work with, stretching his identity to include the ability to lead.

As Vishnu took over the steering wheel, he experienced interior tension; his ability to make his own rules conflicted with his sensitivity to the impact his actions had on others. A CEO must take courses of action that don't yet have clear, set parameters, and thus are difficult to judge. He must transcend common sense to create a new reality not yet on the map. But Vishnu had the ADD quality of interpersonal intuition in spades; he felt guilty both about abandoning his childhood roots and about how those he was leaving in the dust must feel. His interpersonal intuition made it difficult for him to integrate the advantages that his many gifts conferred on him. This dynamic had followed him his entire life, leading him to turn to marijuana to bring him down to the speed, pace, and intelligence of those around him. This pot smoking had prevented him from taking the developmental leap he needed to make—the same one that Prince Hal makes in becoming King Henry IV in the Shakespeare drama. In this classic drama of leadership, Prince Hal must transform his self-image and his social circle of fun-loving troublemakers and assume the mantle of power and royalty. Vishnu needed to follow suit and leave behind the Falstaffs (the central jovial party companion to Prince Hal) of his life. Many gifted kids and adults turn to drug use to drown out feelings of power, charisma, and intelligence. It's a way of punishing themselves for allowing thoughts of superiority to cross their mind—and Vishnu grew up on a commune where such a thought would be heretical. To get a sense of Vishnu's transformation, let's follow his development from childhood to the point where he was struggling to see himself as a poet CEO.

Early Years: Commune Life

Vishnu was born amidst the chaos of 1968 to anarchist revolutionaries living the antiwar lifestyle in the lower east side of Manhattan. His early years consisted of being shuffled from one political rally to the next and multiple trips cross-country, from commune to commune in a funky VW van.

After the peace movement quieted down, his parents chose to lead a spiritual life, living in ashrams on the East and West Coasts. As a result of this alternative lifestyle, Vishnu never attended traditional schools; instead he was taught by various brilliant and loving members of the community, many with advanced degrees in their fields.

Because of this unique environment, Vishnu's ADD didn't hinder his intellectual progress at all; his mind was cultivated and developed by a thoughtful curriculum tailored to his interests, ranging from world history to creative arts, from existential philosophy to metaphysics. He learned at his own pace and was consistently challenged by both new information and unique learning opportunities.

Reentry: The Beginning of the Problem

Right before high school, during his final year of junior high at a Buddhist monastery in Northern California, Vishnu felt a strong desire to "reenter," that is, to fit in with mainstream American society. After so many years of living in a subculture, he felt he lacked critical skills and was not able to participate in society as fully as he wished.

Despite his family's concern, Vishnu enrolled in high school in a rural town north of San Francisco. It was then that his ADD challenges began. He was clearly different than his classmates, better educated and more politically and culturally aware, but also hyperactive and distracted.

Immersed in a traditional learning model after years of teaching tailored to him, Vishnu quickly began to fail basic subjects such as geography and math. His inability to keep quiet and sit still earned him the label of troublemaker and many visits to the principal's office; his arguments with teachers about word etymologies and historical inaccuracies only further compounded their perception that he was a problem child.

He was also socially awkward, unable to fit in with the primarily rural student body. And because the various hippie kids shunned each other in a desperate attempt not to be labeled as the "other," Vishnu felt he had little choice but to modify his personality to be accepted. Easy access to pot through his alternative connections provided the answer. By smoking pot he slowed his mind down and connected with others more easily; by being a source of "good stuff" he became popular with a variety of social groups including stoners, Goths, punks, and even the athletes and farmers' kids. Daily pot use canceled out much of the social and intellectual impact of ADD, allowing him to more easily sync with others; he embraced it with gusto.

But drug use did little to improve his grades or his reputation as a troublemaker. At one point his guidance counselor recommended welding or some other form of vocational training, as a university education seemed far out of reach. An ugly divorce at home only accelerated Vishnu's feelings of isolation and his desire to replace complex, overwhelming emotions with the warm comforting buzz of a good high.

All was not lost, however. His high school had recently received a grant from the state to build one of the most advanced computer labs in the country. This empty room of computers became Vishnu's refuge from the complexity of his life, the flickering glow of the amber CRTs soothing his mind. Word processors helped him with his spelling and grammatical mistakes, allowing him to better compose his thoughts. As a result, his grades began to climb—especially in English and humanities courses—and he graduated on time with decent grades.

The First Awakening: San Francisco

After a stint at community college, he enrolled in a respected university in San Francisco. Here the socially awkward stoner boy found himself among his own kind. It was as if every ADD person on the planet had moved to San Francisco and set up shop. His life exploded: women found him attractive, teachers liked his ideas, and he flourished.

The university's unstructured, build-your-own curriculum model was perfect for Vishnu's intellectual curiosity; he racked up credit after credit in courses in English, religion, film, journalism, linguistics, and anthropology. At the same time, his voracious appetite for drugs was finally sated by partying in the surreal and sublime Haight-Ashbury and Mission districts. In this new environment, his ADD need to seek high levels of stimulation was easily met and he was completely at home; he flourished.

The Choice: A Creative or Corporate Life

During this period of time, Vishnu had to make a critical choice. He had always envisioned himself pursuing an academic or literary career, but his lack of focus wasn't well suited to the years of study these required. He also dabbled in journalism, but his strong empathy for his subject denied him the objectivity required of successful reporters.

He spoke to me of his frustration with one student assignment, in which he had been sent to the Marin Court to report on a drug trial: "Seeing the poor guy up on the stand, stating his case in almost broken English, knowing that he was facing five years in prison, was too much for me to bear. I walked out of the courtroom and threw my notebook away—I couldn't be a part of that system. To have to face those stories would have destroyed me."

The flickering glow of computers offered another choice. Impressed by his sales and technical work at the campus computer store, a leading technology company recruited him to evangelize their newly developed product to students and faculty. This early insight into the emerging Silicon Valley culture came from doors opened by his ADD. Like many people with ADD, when Vishnu found his passion he became over-the-top exhilarated to talk to others about it. He found that he was an articulate evangelist and communicator, able to tailor his message and level of technical detail to his audience. And so he left the world of poets and hippies and jumped into the emerging technological revolution, becoming a highly paid tech consultant.

European Wanderings

After college Vishnu spent four years traveling aimlessly around Europe, using his technical skills to fund a swath of hedonistic behavior, first in London and later in eastern Europe. Playing the role of the wacky California tech wiz kid came easily to him—his ADD only fueled this stereotype. After the fall of the Berlin Wall, he found himself living in eastern Europe, working as a consultant for local and multinational companies.

As an independent technology expert, clients paid a premium for his expertise in markets that were still struggling with basics such as putting food on the table and keeping trains running. But this easy money and his émigré rock-star status led to promiscuity and escalating drug and alcohol use; self-loathing set in. Women were more than happy to offer themselves to the *Amerikanski* businessman, but this felt like cultural exploitation, clashing with his counterculture and feminist upbringing. Feeling that he was taking advantage of the misery and pain of the region, he became deeply depressed. After minor run-ins with organized crime and more than a few jealous boyfriends, Vishnu returned home to California.

The Internet Revolution: ADD Heaven

In the mid-1990s, the San Francisco Bay Area was in a deep recession. Vishnu's unusual work experience didn't lend itself well to steady employment. After months of searching for a technology job, he was offered a low-level position working in a computer store.

After his heady days as a high-flying European consultant, the idea of fixing students' laptops for $12.50 an hour was hard to swallow. Questioning decisions and speaking out of turn, he ran into challenges with teammates and superiors; again he was seen as a troublemaker.

Vishnu gritted his teeth and did his best to make do. Then, in the fall of 1993, he downloaded a new experimental application from the National Center for Supercomputing Applications called Mosaic, and his entire world was transformed. Mosaic, a hypertext-based document model, worked exactly the way his brain did; its branching interconnections allowed him to surf academic and literary documents for hours (this was long before today's Internet).

This early embracing of Internet technology made him once more a recruiting target for leading technology companies. In 1996, he left his low-level job to become, again, a technology evangelist, a dream job for a technologically minded ADD person. For years, Vishnu literally flew around the world preaching the gospel of the Internet, riding the wave of what was perhaps the most powerful explosion of ideas and technology in living memory.

But as much as he enjoyed his role as spokesperson, he started to realize that the real decisions were being made by other kinds of people, with other skills. These people weren't passionate and energetic communicators, they were thoughtful and controlled product managers and executives. He was just a mouthpiece; he wasn't calling the shots. So he set out to acquire new skills.

He moved into product management and spent years developing his organization and time-management skills, both previously weak areas for him. And, perhaps the hardest lesson of all, he started to learn to listen. To be the pitchman was easy, but to listen to customers and engineers—necessary to understand the complex organizational dynamics of a corporation—was really hard. And most importantly, erratic, disruptive behavior that could be tolerated in a technology contractor wouldn't fly in senior management. He needed to change.

Leaving his leading technology position, Vishnu went to a major media company's Internet division, where he quickly rose, first to vice president and then to general manager, with a large staff and significant power. Here, although he was extremely productive and led his team to deliver miracles, he also came into regular conflict with peers and superiors. Either you clicked with Vishnu and loved him, or you didn't and deeply hated him. Regardless, his high output and his ability to deliver impressed his superiors; he was steadily promoted and given ever more responsibility.

The Dark Years: Spackling over the Cracks

The Internet crash of the late 1990s hit Vishnu hard. His executive position evaporated and his multimillion-dollar stock portfolio vanished in a matter of weeks. He was out of work for many months. His reputation as difficult to work with made finding employment in the brutal crash environment impossible; he lived off consulting work and his remaining savings. Working from home, his drug use increased. He was always high; every night he crashed hard on the couch in front of the TV.

Through sheer force of will he picked himself up and got a staff position at one of his old stomping grounds, a leading technology company. After two years of good work there, he took a midlevel management position at a hot start-up and began his climb once again.

But still he ran into problems. He came into conflict with colleagues and superiors. Unwilling to compromise, he would openly defy his bosses. He lost his temper with staffers and acted out in meetings. He increasingly felt that his best years were behind him, that he was all washed-up. Instead of being the founder of a company—as many of his former colleagues were at this point—he was only a midlevel executive, taking orders from people he considered less qualified.

Ultimately his acting out created a toxic environment, polarizing him against colleagues, and he decided to leave. He wanted to start his own company, but he knew he'd only be able to do so if he first got help for his ADD and drug use. His self-esteem in tatters and his career in jeopardy, he began to look for a helping hand.

Recent Realizations: The Gift of ADD

It was at this juncture that Vishnu came to see me. As he tells it, through our work together he came to "a strong realization that the way my brain is wired is both the source of many good things in my life and the source of the conflicts and appetites that have haunted me throughout my life." The realization that his was a hardware problem, not a software problem, relieved much of the anguish and self-loathing that had plagued him. It didn't absolve him of responsibility for his actions, but it did help him understand the root cause of his problems. He wasn't bad or immoral, he just needed to approach life in a different way.

Vishnu immediately started making dramatic changes in his lifestyle and ways of interacting with others and saw extremely rapid results. After twenty-five years of smoking pot, he quit. He began to lay the groundwork to start his own company, working with a leading venture capital company. He also welcomed into his life a new, loving relationship with an attractive, creative woman.

The Poet CEO: An Unstoppable Force

One of the areas that Vishnu and I focused on was the idea of a "poet CEO" as the integration of the two major themes in Vishnu's life—the creative, impulsive, emotional spirit and the organized, disciplined warrior. After working through his self-doubt and self-loathing—by exploring new ways to understand his brain's structure and inner workings—Vishnu is now able to control his emotions and impulsivity. As a result, he can focus his energy in a directed and powerful way.

Vishnu is presently incorporating his company—as the CEO. He is no longer a distracted, hyperactive visionary, but a leader and warrior, and is on track to launch his new technology service in mid-2008 with the backing of a leading venture capital firm in Silicon Valley.

What China Needs Now

Vishnu's story is fascinating not only for the dramatic transformation it shows us, but also for what it reveals about creativity. In *The World Is Flat* (2006a), Thomas Friedman explains that the Chinese have recently realized that they haven't yet figured out how to educate their citizens to create new technologies. Although their education system produces highly competent engineers, if they cannot crank out technology creators, they will be forever beholden to centers of technological innovation like the United States. In some ways, what China is trying to figure out is how to create people like Vishnu. Part of the answer lies in the very gifts of ADD. Notably, Vishnu's childhood on a commune protected him from the difficulties ADD children face daily in the standard school system. As a result, his creative, intuitive exuberance was allowed to flourish during his earliest years. His success is also notable: he is poised to lead a creative technology company in Silicon Valley, the heart of the Internet technology revolution. He is exactly what China is looking for from its own populace. If there is a formula in here, not punishing ADD kids for their daydreams and hyperactivity is one of its key components.

The other revelation of Vishnu's story is his rapid transformation into a leader. The speed of his transformation suggests that it may be easier to teach a creative person the basic skills of focus, organization, and discipline than to teach a high-level fact-finder with powerful organizational skills how to be an inventor-genius.

Vishnu's story can be an inspiration to you. The simple shift to finding and embracing your gifts can lead to dramatic changes. I tremble to think what would have happened if Vishnu had found himself in the mental health system with diagnoses ranging from ADD to cannabis dependence, plus a few oppositional defiant traits hurled at him. (Many psychologists are wont to identify their clients with "traits" of disorders when their clients present with a number of symptoms but don't meet the full criteria for a diagnosis.) A treatment provider would probably have recited well-worn mantras about needing to hit bottom to take care of his pot-smoking habit, and would probably have forced him to acknowledge his powerlessness, not embrace his power. Vishnu didn't need to hit bottom, he needed to see his own light. The cannabis was nothing more than the bushel under which he was hiding it. I reflected that light back to him, giving him permission to share his gifts with the world, and as I did, he no longer needed the cannabis. My diagnosis for Vishnu? Poet CEO with traits of Renaissance man and Enlightenment intellectual—of course, these labels are not in the *Diagnostic and Statistical Manual of Mental Disorders.*

SUMMARY

By way of summary, I have elaborated five gifts of ADD: intense emotional sensitivity, creativity, exuberance, interpersonal intuition, and ecological consciousness. The spaciness, untidiness, and difficulty following instructions typical of ADD may all be related to an intense emotional sensitivity. Similarly, ADD's hyperactivity can be seen as an excess of exuberance or enthusiasm. (A mighty irritant for those resigned to plod through life!)

ADD adults' interpersonal intuition allows them to capture the complexities of interpersonal interactions that can be lost in rational analysis. Indeed, it may well be that it is only our society's insistence on focused clarity, achievement, organization, and rigid schedules that leads us to consider this attention deficit a disorder.

As the other chapters clarified, ADD may actually represent a different way of being in the world, a style of consciousness that *is* different from the normal modern consciousness. In chapter 6 I reviewed the important ecological aspects of ADD and speculated that it could offer a solution to the ecological destruction occurring as a result of current planetary threats. If the normal mode of consciousness is directly responsible for this growing ecological crisis, the promise inherent in ADD is profound. From this perspective, ADD's different style of consciousness may not be a disorder but a movement away from an outmoded way of being in the world.

During my interviews, I was struck by the intense life force of each person I profiled. Whereas others are more composed and put together, these people all had an exuberance that could hardly be contained, making the rest of the world grayer in comparison. If you apply even just some of this book to your life, I am confident you can translate your ADD into a gift that looks more like an evolutionary leap than a mental disorder.

Final Thoughts

I have taken to referring to the gifts of ADD as "the ADD zone." For every person the profile of these gifts will be different; you probably already know what your ADD zone is. It's the work or play you do that feels just right, the activities that you can breeze through with little resistance. For many it is challenging work that allows the opportunity to create, mix it up, or take frequent breaks to physically move around. It is essential that you give yourself permission to live your life almost entirely in your ADD zone.

Spending time outside your ADD zone will cause physical, mental, and emotional depletion. Many ADD adults struggle with depression. Sometimes this is a result of internalizing a punitive stance toward what looks like lazy, sloppy behavior. Often it is due to the depletion of trying too hard to fit in.

I invite you to begin to reshape your life so you can act, move, relate, and live within your own personal ADD zone. This means giving yourself permission to mix it up, live outside the box, and, most of all, respect your big ideas. The ADD adult tends to be a Renaissance man or woman, generating lots of ideas across many domains. This is the opposite of specialization—amassing more and more data on narrower and narrower subjects, or as many have taken to describing it, "knowing more and more about less and less." ADD adults like to know more and more about more and more.

Living in your ADD zone means finding ways to cultivate your ideas. It means not feeling guilt for what you cannot do. One woman sheepishly reported that she enjoyed parenting more after she got divorced and had shared custody arrangements. This bit of mixing it up met some of her basic needs and increased her enjoyment of parenting. Ask yourself, "What do I need to realize to stop feeling guilty?" Generate as many possible answers as you can. Some answers that may help include the following:

- I need to realize that I'm different because I'm ahead of the curve, not because I'm stupid.

- I need to realize that others don't benefit from me feeling guilty.

- I need to realize that others don't want me to feel guilty.

- I need to realize that I have a right to stand up for my own personal style.

- I need to realize that doing things beyond normal expectations is high-level problem solving.

- I need to realize that acting without full analysis of costs is part of how I'm hardwired.

- I need to realize that I am more than my ADD.

- I need to realize that I have permission to live inside my ADD zone.

- I need to realize that I can't possibly do it all.

- I need to realize that I can't possibly live up to others' expectations.

- I need to realize that my big ideas are my treasures.

These are just to get you started. Write out as many possible answers as you can. Use these phrases to ask for what you need in your relationships. Advocate for yourself.

SUPPORT GROUPS

One concrete step toward meeting your needs is to start a support group with other ADD adults. This could be as simple as a book group that uses this book as a resource. The following is a guide for structuring your group:

1. Share, cultivate, and honor big ideas.

2. Help each other translate symptoms into needs.

3. Help each other solve the problem of getting needs met.

4. Support each other with resources.

One of the biggest gifts of ADD is that it forces you to realize that you cannot do it all alone. You will need support along the way; use this book as a centerpiece for creating a supportive community. This will give you the opportunity to tap into the incredible resources and gifts of others—and this, in turn, will help you generously share your own gifts with the world.

It may help to remember what is at stake: Your gifts are not just for you. The world needs your gifts. Your family, your friends, your community, and your world need you to stop beating yourself up, playing small, and feeling guilty about what you cannot do.

Learn More About Dr. Lara Honos-Webb's Work

Explore Dr. Lara Honos-Webb's other books, learning programs, seminars, and professional training to reinforce and advance what you've learned in this book. Sign up for Dr. Lara Honos-Webb's free newsletter at www.visionarysoul.com/newsletter.html. More details can be found at www.visionarysoul.com.

SEMINARS AND TRAINING

Dr. Lara Honos-Webb provides world-class training programs for organizations, hospitals, health care providers, and individuals. A sample of workshop and seminar titles includes the following:

- The Gift of ADHD
- Listening to Depression: How Understanding Your Pain Can Heal Your Life
- Parenting with Passion: Do What You Love, the Kids Will Follow
- Marriage Minders: A Revolutionary New Approach to Preventing Marital Blowouts

- Translate Your Pain into Purpose: An Alternative Mental Health Revolution
- Points on the Board, Oil Changes, and Tune-Ups: Getting Your Hubby to Sign On to Marital Bliss on His Own Terms
- What's Right with My Child?
- How to Deal with Challenging Behavior in Your Child
- ADHD in the Workplace
- Depression in the Workplace
- Create Emotional Intelligence in the Workplace

BOOKS AND E-BOOKS

Books

The Gift of ADHD Activity Book: 101 Ways to Turn Your Child's Problems into Strengths. Oakland, CA: New Harbinger Publications, 2008.

Listening to Depression: How Understanding Your Pain Can Heal Your Life. Oakland, CA: New Harbinger Publications, 2006.

The Gift of ADHD: How to Transform Your Child's Problems into Strengths. Oakland, CA: New Harbinger Publications, 2005.

E-Books

When Self-Help Hurts: Letting Go of Seeking by Finding Yourself

This powerful e-book will help you to stop seeking and begin finding. The simple pursuit of transformation has the effect of making you a seeker. The creation of your destiny is playful art. Its grandeur will be found in its breathtaking originality, not in any technical perfection beaten into it through years of reform school. Available at www.visionarysoul.com.

Learning the Art of Giving Yourself Permission

This e-book reviews the healing power of giving yourself permission rather than yet more demands. Transform your romantic and professional life and increase your capacity to let go and have fun by practicing giving yourself permission. Available at www.visionarysoul.com.

Parenting with Passion: Do What You Love, the Children Will Follow

Parents don't have to give up what they love, even when raising young children. This e-book will show you how to find and follow your bliss while giving your kids everything they need and more. Available at www.visionarysoul.com.

The Psychology of Pregnancy and Birth

This e-book explores the dramatic life changes women experience during pregnancy and prepares them for birth and that transition to motherhood. Available at www.visionarysoul.com.

References

Abrahamson, E., and D.H. Freedman. 2007. *A Perfect Mess: The Hidden Benefits of Disorder—How Crammed Closets, Cluttered Offices, and On-the-Fly Planning Make the World a Better Place.* New York: BackBay Books.

Allen, M. 2006. *The Type Z Guide to Success: A Lazy Person's Manifesto for Wealth and Fulfillment.* Novato, CA: New World Library.

American Academy of Child and Adolescent Psychiatry. 2007. Practice parameters for the assessment and treatment of children and adolescents with attention-deficit/hyperactivity disorder. Retrieved from www.guideline.gov/summary/summary.aspx?ss=15&doc_id=11375&nbr=5912 on January 9, 2008.

American Psychiatric Association. 2000. *Diagnostic and Statistical Manual of Mental Disorders,* 4th ed, text revision. Washington, DC: American Psychiatric Association.

Barkley, R.A. 2000. *Taking Charge of ADHD: The Complete Authoritative Guide for Parents.* New York: Guilford Press.

Barkley, R.A., K.R. Murphy, and M. Fischer. 2008. *ADHD in Adults: What the Science Says.* New York: Guilford Press.

Briggs, J. 2000. *Fire in the Crucible: Understanding the Process of Creative Genius.* Grand Rapids, MI: Phanes Press.

Buckingham, M., and D.O. Clifton. 2001. *Now, Discover Your Strengths.* New York: Free Press.

Byrne, R. 2006. *The Secret.* New York: Simon and Schuster.

Comaford-Lynch, C. 2007. *Rules for Renegades.* New York: McGraw Hill.

Diller, L. 2006. *The Last Normal Child: Essays on the Intersection of Kids, Culture, and Psychiatric Drugs.* Westport, CT: Praeger Publishers.

Freud, S. 1963. *Therapy and Technique.* New York: Collier.

Friedman, T. 2006. *The World Is Flat: A Brief History of the Twenty-First Century.* New York: Farrar, Straus, and Giroux.

_____. 2006. Interview by Tim Russert. *Tim Russert,* MSNBC, July 22.

Gottman, J., J. Murray, C. Swanson, R. Tyson, and K. Swanson. 2002. *The Mathematics of Marriage.* Cambridge, MA: MIT Press.

Hallowell, E.M., and J.J. Ratey. 1994. *Driven to Distraction.* New York: Simon and Schuster.

_____. 2005. *Delivered from Distraction: Getting the Most out of Life with Attention Deficit Disorder.* New York: Ballantine Books.

Harris, B. 2007. *The Fire and the Rose: The Wedding of Spirituality and Sexuality.* Wilmette, IL: Chiron.

Hazell, C. 2003. *The Experience of Emptiness.* Bloomington, IN: 1st Books Library.

Hillman, J. 1983. *Healing Fiction.* New York: Station Hill.

_____. 1996. *The Soul's Code: In Search of Character and Calling.* New York: Random House.

Hillman, J., and M. Ventura. 1992. *We've Had a Hundred Years of Psychotherapy and the World's Getting Worse.* New York: HarperCollins.

Honos-Webb, L. 2005. *The Gift of ADHD: How to Transform Your Child's Problems into Strengths.* Oakland, CA: New Harbinger Publications.

______. 2006. *Listening to Depression: How Understanding Your Pain Can Heal Your Life.* Oakland, CA: New Harbinger Publications.

______. 2008. *The Gift of ADHD Activity Book: 101 Ways to Transform Problems into Strengths.* Oakland, CA: New Harbinger Publications.

Jenkins, D. 2005. *Dream RePlay: How to Transform Your Dream Life.* Oakland, CA: Booklocker.com.

Kessler, R. C. 2006. The prevalence and correlates of adult ADHD in the United States: Results from the National Comorbidity Survey Replication. *American Journal of Psychiatry* 163:716–723.

Lamberg, L. 2003. ADHD often undiagnosed in adults: Appropriate treatment may benefit work, family, social life. *Journal of the American Medical Association* 290(12):1565–1567.

Levine, M. 2006. *The Price of Privilege: How Parental Pressure and Material Advantage Are Creating a Generation of Disconnected and Unhappy Kids.* San Francisco: HarperCollins.

Lewis, T., F. Amini, and R. Lannon, R. 2000. *A General Theory of Love.* New York Random House.

Madson, P.R. 2005. *Improv Wisdom: Don't Prepare, Just Show Up.* New York: Random House.

McCrae, R.R. 1987. Creativity, divergent thinking, and openness to experience. *Journal of Personality and Social Psychology* 52(6):1258–1265.

Moynihan, R., and A. Cassels. 2002. *Selling Sickness.* New York: Avalon.

Orfalea, P. 2007. *Copy This! How I Turned Dyslexia, ADHD, and 100 Square Feet into a Company Called Kinko's.* New York: Workman.

Pink, D.H. 2005. *A Whole New Mind.* New York: Penguin.

Ponder, C. 1962. *The Dynamic Laws of Prosperity.* Marina del Rey, CA: DeVorss & Co.

Reik, T. 1948. *Listening with the Third Ear: The Inner Experience of a Psychoanalyst.* New York: Farrar, Straus and Giroux.

Rice, L.N., and Greenberg, L.S. 1984. *Patterns of Change: Intensive Analysis of Psychotherapy Process.* New York: Guilford Press.

Sarkis, S.M. 2006. *10 Simple Solutions to Adult ADD: How to Overcome Chronic Distraction and Accomplish Your Goals.* Oakland, CA: New Harbinger Publications.

______. 2008. *Making the Grade with ADD: A Student's Guide to Succeeding in College with Attention Deficit Disorder.* Oakland, CA: New Harbinger Publications.

Taylor, A.F., F.E. Kuo, and W.C. Sullivan. 2001. Coping with ADD: The surprising connection to green play settings. *Environment and Behavior* 33:54–77.

Tolstoy, L. 2003. *The Death of Ivan Ilyich and Other Stories.* New York: Signet Classics.

Turner, R.A., M. Altemus, D.N. Yip, E. Kupferman, D. Fletcher, A. Bostrom, D.M. Lyons, and J.A. Amico. 2002. Effects of emotion on oxytocin, prolactin, and ACTH in women. *Stress* 5(4):269–276.

Wallis, C., and S. Steptoe. 2006. How to bring our schools out of the 20th century. *Time Magazine,* December 18, 51–56.

About the Author

Lara Honos-Webb, Ph.D., is a clinical psychologist licensed in California. Her work has been featured in *Newsweek,* ivillage.com, msn.com, abcnews.com, the *Wall Street Journal,* the *Chicago Tribune,* and *Publisher's Weekly,* as well as newspapers across the country and national radio and television programs. Her book, *Listening to Depression* was selected by *Health* magazine as one of the best therapy books of 2006. Her books have over 125,000 copies in print. The American Psychological Association included *The Gift of ADHD* in its recommended reading list in their "ADHD Parents Medication Guide." She specializes in the treatment of ADHD, depression, and the psychology of pregnancy and motherhood, and speaks regularly on her areas of expertise. Honos-Webb completed a two-year postdoctoral research fellowship at University of California, San Francisco, and has taught graduate students as an assistant professor. She has published more than twenty-five scholarly articles. Visit her website at www.visionarysoul.com.

Image I

Books For ALL Kinds of Readers

At ReadHowYouWant we understand that one size does not fit all types of readers. Our innovative, patent pending technology allows us to design new formats to make reading easier and more enjoyable for you. This helps improve your speed of reading and your comprehension. Our EasyRead printed books have been optimized to improve word recognition, ease eye tracking by adjusting word and line spacing as well as minimizing hyphenation. Our EasyRead SuperLarge editions have been developed to make reading easier and more accessible for vision-impaired readers. We offer Braille and DAISY formats of our books and all popular E-Book formats.

Printed in Dunstable, United Kingdom

91341971R00203